D0054074

Biography

Louisa May ALCOTT

Amy Ruth

Lerner Publications Company
Minneapolis

This book is dedicated with love and thanks to my husband, Jim Meisner; my mother, Martha Lee Rhodes; and my sister, Melissa Ruth. Special thanks also must go to author and historian Mary J. Bennett for inspiration and support, and to the Theresa W. Pratt Trust for permission to quote from the letters, diaries, and works of Louisa May Alcott.

Lerner Publications Company
241 First Avenue North
Minneapolis, MN 55401

Website address: www.lernerbooks.com

Library of Congress Cataloging-in-Publication Data

Ruth, Amy.
    Louisa May Alcott / by Amy Ruth.
    p. cm. — (A & E biography)
    Summary: Discusses the life of the popular nineteenth-century author who wrote "Little Women."
    ISBN 0-8225-4938-7 (alk. paper)
    1. Alcott, Louisa May, 1832–1888—Juvenile literature.
    2. Women authors, American —19th century—Biography—Juvenile literature. [1. Alcott, Louisa May, 1832–1888.
    2. Authors, American. 3. Women—Biography.] I. Title. II. Series.
PS1018.R87 1999
813'.4
[B]—dc21   97-47283

Manufactured in the United States of America
1 2 3 4 5 6 – JR – 04 03 02 01 00 99

CONTENTS

Like Louisa, Jo March in Little Women *anxiously sought approval from publishers, as depicted by artist Norman Rockwell in 1938.*

Chapter **ONE**

LOUISA

LOUISA MAY ALCOTT HURRIED THROUGH THE BUSY
Boston streets, clutching a manuscript close to her as
she made her way to the office of publisher James T.
Fields. Fields had published books by well-known
writers such as poet Henry Wadsworth Longfellow
and essayist Ralph Waldo Emerson. In 1850, three
years before Louisa's visit, he had published *The Scarlet Letter,* a novel by Nathaniel Hawthorne.

As Louisa waited nervously amidst the piles of books
and manuscripts in Fields' office, the publisher sat behind a green curtain and reviewed her article care-
fully. When he was done, he observed her seriously
and remarked, "Stick to your teaching, Miss Alcott,
you can't write."

If Louisa had heeded this advice, generations of readers would have been deprived of one of the most famous stories ever written. In 1868, fifteen years after her encounter with James T. Fields, Louisa penned the classic tale *Little Women* and became one of the world's most-loved authors of all time.

Fields's rejection only fueled Louisa's determination. When she left his office, she vowed that she would sell stories to all the prominent publishers in Boston—including James T. Fields. She was right. By the time *Little Women* was published, Louisa May Alcott was a much sought-after writer. Eventually, her beloved children's books earned her the nickname "The Children's Friend."

Louisa May Alcott was born in Germantown, Pennsylvania, on November 29, 1832—her father's thirty-third birthday. Hours after she was born, her father announced her arrival in a letter to his father-in-law, Colonel Joseph May of Boston. Amos Bronson Alcott wrote in his letter that he hoped his second daughter would take her place in society and that her name would someday be associated with "exalted worth."

Bronson, as he was known, was proud of his growing family. Just a year and a half earlier, he and his wife, Abigail May Alcott, had had their first daughter, Anna. Bronson was fascinated by human nature and as his two girls grew, he began writing about their development. He hoped to publish his observations in a book someday. He noted that Anna was calm, well

As a young child, Louisa was already strong-willed.

behaved, and pleasant. He admired these qualities very much. Louisa, on the other hand, was a lively, temperamental child and, Bronson believed, very much like her mother. Abigail, affectionately known as Abba, had a passionate nature. "[Louisa] is more active . . . than Anna," Bronson wrote. "Anna is ideal, sentimental. Louisa is practical, energetic."

Louisa also had physical traits that Bronson disliked—a dark olive complexion and mischievous dark gray eyes. Although he actively opposed slavery, Bronson associated darker skin and eyes with a less desirable personality. Louisa looked like her mother's relatives, the Mays, who may have descended from Portuguese Jews.

It was understood that Anna was Bronson's favorite daughter. Still, even though he sometimes did not know how to relate to the daughter who shared his birthday, he loved Louisa dearly. As she grew, traits of both Bronson and Abba emerged in her. Louisa's fiery temper and Mediterranean looks came from her mother, while her determination to live as she wished came from her father.

A self-educated man from a poor family, Bronson was a born teacher. He intended to make a living by running his own school, where he could put his forward-thinking ideas into practice. At the time, schools were very structured and strict. Students learned by memorizing huge amounts of information, which they repeated back to their teacher. Bronson did not think children learned well by memorization. He wanted his students to understand what they learned rather than just repeat it by rote.

In the early to mid-1800s, many people, like Bronson Alcott, worked to reform education in the United States. The reform movement happened as Americans' ideas about childhood were changing. Parents, especially mothers, became more involved in their children's lives. It was no longer considered appropriate to leave their care in the hands of servants and hired governesses and tutors. Children dressed in more comfortable clothes, which allowed them to play and explore freely. Parents encouraged their children to develop as individuals and no longer modeled them to be little adults.

Nineteenth-century reformers pushed for the construction of public schools. They wanted all children to learn not only academic subjects, but also good moral behavior, which traditionally had been taught in the home and church. As increasing numbers of children attended school, reformers rewrote textbooks and organized colleges to instruct men and women how to be good teachers. By the 1850s, many states had free public school systems. In 1852, Massachusetts was the first state to pass a compulsory education law, requiring children aged eight to fourteen to attend school for at least three months each year. Other states followed with similar laws. Between the 1840s and 1870s, more and more Americans were learning to read and write. In some states, literacy rates rose from 75 percent to between 91 and 97 percent.

In 1834, Bronson moved his family to Boston, Massachusetts, where he started the Temple School. He received help from Elizabeth Peabody, a scholar from a wealthy, influential family who liked Bronson's teaching methods. He held lively classroom discussions to encourage individual thought. Instead of following a strict schedule, the way more traditional teachers did, he made each school day different. He taught from the books of great authors and philosophers instead of using traditional textbooks. One of Bronson's favorite books was *Pilgrim's Progress,* a story about humanity's journey toward goodness. He believed children should be guided through life and given the tools to make the right choices. Bronson also taught sex education and opened his school to all races. These educational methods have become standard, but in Bronson's time they were radical.

For a time, the school was a success. When the Alcotts' third daughter was born in 1835, they named her Elizabeth after the woman who had brought Bronson's methods to the public. They called the baby "Lizzie" for short.

For Louisa's third birthday and Bronson's thirty-sixth, Bronson and Abba arranged a celebration at the Temple School. The students crowned Louisa with a wreath of leaves, and everyone enjoyed recitations of poems, essays, and stories. The birthday girl was asked to pass out refreshments. As Louisa watched the little plum cakes disappear one by one into the hands of other children, she soon realized that there were more children than cakes. She clutched the last cake to herself but was gently reminded that it was better to give than to receive. Bronson taught his girls—often by example—that self-sacrifice was the path to goodness. One winter, he gave away his family's supply of firewood to a family that was poorer than the Alcotts.

When his daughters were old enough to read, Bronson celebrated their birthdays with a yearly letter in which he praised their good qualities and encouraged them to resolve their imperfections.

Louisa was happy in Boston. "One of my earliest memories is of playing with books in my father's study," she later wrote. "Building towers and bridges of the big dictionaries, looking at pictures, pretending to read, and scribbling on blank pages whenever pen or

At the Temple School, Bronson taught his students to understand rather than simply repeat new information.

pencil could be found." She also enjoyed rolling her hoop around Boston Common, exploring the bustling streets, and playing in a frog pond. Once, the adventurous Louisa fell into a pond and was rescued by a black boy. About meeting her first black friend, Louisa remarked, "I was an abolitionist at the age of three."

The antislavery or abolition movement was another important reform effort of the nineteenth century. Slavery in America dated back to the 1600s, when African men, women, and children were kidnapped from their homes, taken to the states, and sold as

Louisa enjoyed playing in Boston Common.

slaves. The economy of the Southern colonies, based mainly on the cotton industry, depended on slave labor. A political rift formed between Northern colonies, where slavery was outlawed, and Southern colonies, which defended slavery.

Abolitionists like the Alcotts opposed slavery. Abolitionists published many newspapers and pamphlets detailing the horrors of slavery. They also lectured, lobbied lawmakers, and supported the Underground Railroad, a series of safe hideaways where runaway slaves could find food and shelter in their journey to freedom from the southern United States to Canada.

Bronson educated his daughters at home, teaching them in the same way he taught his Temple School students. "Walks each morning . . . were a part of our education, as well as every sort of housework," Louisa remembered. Bronson and Abba taught their girls to be self-reliant, practical, and independent during a time when much of society did not believe in preparing girls to lead independent lives. Although increasing numbers of girls attended school in the 1840s and 1850s, they were still trained to be better mothers and wives, rather than to have jobs or careers outside the home. Some educators believed that girls' brains were weaker than boys' and did not let girls study subjects such as math and science. Women and girls who pursued studies in these areas were often ridiculed.

Although Bronson was strict, he wanted his daughters to have fun. He let them have spirited pillow fights at bedtime and encouraged them to read for pleasure.

In 1836, a Boston publisher agreed to publish some of the conversations Bronson and his students had in the classroom. When parents and community members realized that Bronson was teaching students about childbirth and untraditional views of religion, they were horrified. Parents, embarrassed to be associated with Bronson Alcott, withdrew their students from the Temple School. The failure of the school was a major blow for Bronson, and he became despondent.

No students meant no income for Bronson. Soon people to whom he owed money demanded payment, but he had no money to pay them. Abba's family tried to persuade her to leave her husband. The Mays were a prominent Boston family, and they did not want their name connected with a radical philosopher who couldn't support his wife and children. Abba remained devoted to her husband, however.

Bronson Alcott

Chapter **TWO**

CONCORD AND TRANSCENDENTALISM

AFTER THE FAILURE OF THE TEMPLE SCHOOL IN 1836, the Alcotts fell into hard times. Bronson could no longer find teaching jobs in Boston. He decided to hold "philosophical conversations," or lectures followed by discussions, on topics such as materialism, poetry, and the mystery of life. Unfortunately, few people paid to hear him speak.

By this time, Bronson had become deeply devoted to a new way of thinking called transcendentalism. Bronson's ideas about universal goodness, self-sacrifice, and simple living were similar to the transcendentalist philosophy. Discouraged by the Temple School failure, he was drawn to the hope he saw in transcendentalism.

Followers of this school of thought believed that

people were born with a knowledge that "transcended," or went beyond, the five senses and allowed them to know instinctively what was good and right. Transcendentalists believed in living simply, surrounded by nature, and in pursuing knowledge and justice. These reformers thought that Americans were too materialistic—caring more about material things than the spiritual life. Although transcendentalism as a movement was active for only a short period between the 1830s and the 1860s, it had a tremendous lasting effect. One of the most important transcendentalists was Ralph Waldo Emerson, whose writings and reflections influenced many great American writers, including Henry David Thoreau, Walt Whitman, and Emily Dickinson. Emerson is perhaps best known for his essay "Self-Reliance," but he wrote many books and essays and lectured worldwide.

Bronson Alcott met Emerson in 1835, when they were introduced by a mutual friend. They greatly admired one another. Emerson was one of the few people who believed Bronson was a brilliant philosopher. It was Emerson who came to the Alcotts' rescue when the Temple School closed. Emerson lived in a small town eighteen miles west of Boston. Concord, Massachusetts, was famous as the site of the first battle of the Revolutionary War in 1775. Emerson hoped to make Concord famous for its great thinkers as well. He could accomplish this if people like Bronson Alcott moved to the community.

Ralph Waldo Emerson was a devoted and generous friend to the Alcott family.

Abba did not want to move to a small town, where her family's untraditional ways would stand out. She preferred the anonymity of a large city. But she agreed to move to Concord to make her husband happy. In the spring of 1840, with financial help from Abba's relatives, the Alcotts packed up their belongings and moved to a cottage in Concord. Bronson named the place Dove Cottage.

Upon arrival, Bronson set to work fixing up the place and planting a garden. The Alcotts intended to grow their own food and to be as self-sufficient as possible. Bronson made the conscious decision not to work for others for a wage. He believed that Americans were too caught up in earning money and buying things. He did not wish to contribute to the problem by earning and spending money. Bronson did find it acceptable to take donations for his philosophical conversations, but the donations did not amount to much. As a result, the family was forced to rely on donations of food, clothing, and cash from

While living in Dove Cottage, Louisa was influenced by important thinkers and writers of the time.

family members and friends. Emerson often made large anonymous donations to the Alcotts, which kept them, at times, from starving.

Bronson believed in pure living. He wanted his family to be strict vegetarians—eating only grains, fruits, and vegetables—which did not require them to kill a living creature with a soul. Sometimes, however, Abba insisted that her growing daughters have meat. This led to bitter arguments between Louisa's parents. Bronson believed that meat was responsible for Abba's and Louisa's moody temperaments.

Abba supported Bronson in almost all his endeavors, no matter how strange or risky they seemed. She believed in his educational philosophies and his ideas for reform. But when it came to her daughters, Abba Alcott fiercely protected their well-being. Throughout her life, Louisa watched as her parents matched wits and wills, an exercise that often left both of them frustrated and exhausted.

Regardless of the strife, Concord was a special place for Louisa. At a time when girls and women were not generally encouraged to develop their intellectual abilities, Louisa and her sisters spent time with some of the most noted American thinkers and writers of all time. Louisa met intellectual women such as Margaret Fuller, a writer and reformer who was editor of the transcendentalist magazine *The Dial*. Louisa learned at an early age that women were capable of independent thought and action.

The Alcott girls took their school lessons with Bronson, Ralph Waldo Emerson, and Henry David Thoreau, who wrote the most famous transcendentalist work, *Walden.* Louisa especially liked classes in composition, history, and geography. She tried to avoid arithmetic and grammar. Bronson made spelling lessons fun by twisting his body into the shapes of letters.

Most of all, the Alcott girls loved the expansive countryside surrounding their Concord home. Bronson remarked that his daughters often had trouble concentrating on their lessons. "Their thoughts are on the distant hill, the winding river, the orchard, the meadow, or grove," he said. The sisters enjoyed going on berry-picking expeditions with Thoreau, who told mesmerizing stories about forest fairies and elves who lived among the cobwebs and pinecones on the forest floor.

Wild Louisa was a tomboy who befriended neighborhood boys only after she had beaten them in a running race. She had no interest in girls who did not like to run or climb trees. "I always thought I must have been a deer or a horse in some former state, because it was such a joy to run," she said.

In July 1840, when Louisa was seven, the Alcotts welcomed another daughter—Abigail May Alcott—into their family, and the girls had another playmate. The family called the new baby Abby, but later in life she preferred to be called May. The four girls affectionately referred to their mother as "Marmee."

"Marmee" was a constant source of comfort and support for the family.

Bronson required his daughters to record their feelings and observations in a daily journal. Bronson himself kept a journal all his life. Journals were shared among the family members. Louisa especially liked it when her mother peeked into her journal and left behind encouraging words that inspired Louisa to be good, despite her bad temper.

On Louisa's eighth birthday, Bronson again tried to teach her the rewards of goodness and an even temper. His birthday letter to her included pictures of an angel with a harp and an angel with an arrow. Louisa was the angel with the arrow, Bronson said, and she must strive toward the harmony represented by the angel with the harp.

While Louisa worked to improve her temper, a more important quality emerged. During the spring of her eighth year, Louisa wrote her first poem, "To the First Robin."

> Welcome, welcome, little stranger,
> Fear no harm, and fear no danger;
> We are glad to see you here,
> For you sing "Sweet Spring is near."
>
> Now the white snow melts away;
> Now the flowers blossom gay:
> Come dear bird and build your nest,
> For we love our robin best.

Louisa's celebration of nature and her respect for the vulnerable robin reveal that she had embraced her father's philosophy. Louisa may not have succeeded in finding harmony within herself, but she knew how to look for it in nature.

By the time Louisa was ten years old, life was even harder for the Alcotts. Debts had continued to pile up, and Bronson's mood was bleak and desperate. He had been writing for *The Dial,* but his poorly organized articles rambled on, and readers did not understand what Bronson was trying to say. Once again, Abba's family urged her to leave Bronson, but she refused. As much as she resented his unwillingness to support his family by working, Abba loved Bronson with all her heart. Although she was often frustrated and angry with him, she would stand by him in good times and in bad. But she would not stand by and do nothing. She began to take in sewing—she, Anna, and Louisa sewed shirts and linens for money. For the rest of their lives, the Alcott women would support the family.

While Bronson's radical teaching methods were not welcome in the United States, some British educators in England adopted his methods. These teachers agreed with Bronson's belief in stimulating classrooms where students were encouraged to express their own ideas instead of simply memorizing someone else's. In May 1842, Bronson was invited to the Alcott House, a school in London named in his honor. Emerson—the Alcotts' guardian angel—paid Bronson's way.

As Louisa watched her father set sail for England, she had mixed feelings. She knew that life in Dove Cottage would be calmer with Bronson away. But she also knew that she would miss her eccentric and thoughtful father. Perhaps, Louisa hoped, Bronson would return from England a happier man.

At Fruitlands, the Alcotts experimented with communal living.

Chapter **THREE**

FRUITLANDS

DURING THE SIX MONTHS BRONSON WAS IN England, Abba and her daughters busied themselves with lessons and housework. But in August 1842— two months before Bronson's ship docked at Boston Harbor—Louisa and her sisters could wait no longer. They missed Bronson's dynamic presence and wanted to make his return special. They cleaned Dove Cottage until it gleamed and decorated it with garlands of amaranths, chrysanthemums, and other fall flowers.

When he returned to Concord, Bronson was touched and surprised by his family's hard work. He had brought a surprise of his own. Three men—Charles Lane, Lane's son William, and Henry Wright—had come from England with Bronson. Together they would prepare for a new life in a communal society. In a communal society, people worked together toward common goals, such as group self-sufficiency and universal goodness.

The men envisioned a place where they could put their beliefs into practice by living as vegetarians, working only for the common good, and studying the great philosophers. They wanted a place where individuals could purify their bodies and minds and live together as a large "consociate family," united and self-sufficient in every way.

In the 1840s, many people were forming communal societies like the one Bronson hoped to organize. People who formed these communities were responding to what they viewed as societal injustices. They longed to live in a place where all people were equal and everyone's needs were met. These communities were sometimes referred to as utopias or utopian societies, because they strived to create a perfect society.

Like Bronson Alcott, Charles Lane was a philosopher and social reformer. He had a profound impact on the close-knit Alcott family. Life at Dove Cottage began to change almost as soon as the Lanes and Henry Wright moved in with the Alcotts. Charles Lane imposed strict rules concerning diet and routine. He took the joy out of life for Louisa and her sisters.

Bronson took over the preparation of meals, and the family ate apples, bread, cold potatoes, and water. Abba complained that the unripe apples hurt her teeth. Lane instructed the Alcotts not to waste time or energy—so they ate dinner without plates, because plates had to be washed and put away.

Lane conducted philosophical conversations at mealtimes and restricted the free time the Alcott girls had once enjoyed for playing. The girls and William took lessons from Charles beginning early in the morning and continuing into the late afternoon. At night, the six Alcotts slept in one tiny room on the second floor, while Henry Wright used the other second-floor bedroom. Lane and his son enjoyed the comfort of Bronson's first-floor study.

Bronson was so caught up in his new friends that he forgot to give Louisa a present for her tenth birthday. She received only advice in his traditional birthday letter.

"I am almost suffocated in this atmosphere of restriction and reform," Abba wrote in her journal. She poured her exasperation into her journal, and in December, she went to Boston alone for two weeks. She returned resolved to support her husband and his new friends. Although Abba was a strong-willed, intelligent woman, she was much like other wives in the 1800s, who typically deferred to their husbands' wishes and decisions.

During the next few months, the men lectured extensively and began laying the groundwork for their utopian community. Wright eventually left Concord and returned to England. Lane and Bronson scouted the countryside for a suitable site for the "new Eden."

Lane purchased a 100-acre, run-down farmstead tucked away in a remote location near the town of Harvard, Massachusetts.

On June 1, 1843—an unusually cold summer day— the Alcotts and the Lanes packed their belongings into a wagon and moved to the farm. Louisa and her sister Lizzie rode atop the furniture and trunks while the others walked the fifteen miles from Concord. The group trudged along the muddy roads, accompanied by high hopes and a steady rainfall.

Bronson optimistically renamed the drafty, rustic red farmhouse "Fruitlands" in hopes of seeing this experiment in living bear fruit and spread its seed. At first the Alcotts were enchanted by their new home. The fine summer weather and lush countryside swelled with promise. Even Abba, reluctant to leave Concord and unsure of Charles Lane, felt hopeful. During the first week in their new home, Abba and the girls surveyed the property. They took long walks, peeked into the dilapidated barns, and gathered firewood and wildflowers. On June 4, Abba wrote in her journal, "Walked over our little territory of woodland, vale, meadow, and pasture. Hill, grove, forest—all beautiful, the hills commanding one of the most expansive prospects in the country."

Charles Lane and Bronson Alcott knew that if the community was to be self-sufficient, they would need to yield a harvest from their land. Almost immediately—but past the prime planting period—the men

Larger and more successful than Fruitlands, the Oneida Community in New York State was a well-known utopian community in the 1800s.

planted corn, potatoes, carrots, turnips, beans, and other vegetables in the garden, and wheat, barley, and rye in the fields. Apple, cherry, and peach trees promised abundant fruit. Bronson planned to have an even larger orchard eventually. Streams and springs flowed through the meadows and rolling hills. A nearby forest of oak, maple, walnut, and chestnut trees promised fuel, edible roots, berries, and nuts.

Abba and her daughters hoped that Bronson's new venture would succeed and give the family the security it needed.

The number of inhabitants in the community varied, rising at one point to as many as sixteen people. Bronson tried to persuade relatives to join Fruitlands. Although curious relatives and friends did visit, few were bold enough to stay.

The inhabitants of Fruitlands adhered to a strict vegetarian diet, according to Lane's severe rules. He believed it was ungodly to take flesh from any animal, including milk from a cow and eggs from a chicken. Lane taught the children short sayings to remind them that they must resist an animal diet. He believed animal foods polluted human bodies and minds. Louisa copied some of these sayings into her journal, including, "Vegetable diet and sweet repose. Animal food and nightmare." Coffee and tea also were forbidden. Only water—Mother Nature's pure drink—was permitted. One resident at Fruitlands was banished after it was discovered that she had enjoyed a few bites of fish during a visit to a neighbor.

Lane's beliefs about pure living also extended to clothing. Cotton was the product of slave labor in the South, wool rightfully belonged to sheep, and silk was the product of worms. Only linen, made from the flax plant, was a natural material that did not exploit any human or animal. Lane fashioned linen tunics, bloomers, and wide-brimmed hats for the group.

For a while, ten-year-old Louisa felt comfortable, even happy, in her new home. She was used to her father's eccentricities. Besides, she learned that the nearby woods offered a temporary escape from Bronson's and Lane's stern discipline. There, she and her sisters made up games, picked juicy berries and pretty wildflowers, sang cheery songs, and wrote poems for each other. The whole family sometimes went to the woods together to celebrate special occasions with poetry readings and parties.

Louisa was exploring the farmstead one day when she peeked into a brick fireplace. She discovered, to her surprise, that the space was occupied by a young runaway slave. Like Concord, Fruitlands was a stop on the Underground Railroad, the long line of safe houses for runaway slaves.

Still required by her father to keep a daily journal, Louisa spent much time with her thoughts, turning them around and around in her mind. At night in her attic bedroom, Louisa watched the moon in silence and listened to the pitter-patter of the rain. "It made a pretty noise on the roof," she wrote in her journal.

On July 4th, Ralph Waldo Emerson visited Fruitlands. He had been wary of the settlement from the start. Although he had financed some of Bronson's earlier experiments, he would not donate money to this latest scheme. He shared Abba's doubts about Charles Lane. Upon leaving Fruitlands, he noted in his journal that the family was fine in July, when the weather was fair, but he predicted things would be different in December.

Members of Fruitlands were required to live according to a strict schedule. Lane believed in early rising and cold baths. But it would take more than a few cold baths to shake Louisa's spirit. On one occasion, she wrote in her journal, "I love cold water!" Louisa's chores included setting the supper table, washing dishes, sewing, ironing, and looking after May.

In September, just four months after moving to Fruitlands, Louisa was still in high spirits. Stubborn as always, she would not give in to Lane's tyranny. Like most girls her age, Louisa was happy, energetic, and carefree. She did not resemble the calm and gentle girl that Bronson and Lane wanted her to become. The New England countryside continued to inspire her. "I ran in the wind today and played be a horse, and had a lovely time in the woods with Anna and Lizzie," she wrote in her journal. "We were fairies, and made gowns and paper wings."

Louisa and her sisters had school lessons during the day. Under the guidance of Lane and Bronson, they studied writing, spelling, poetry, math, singing, and other subjects. Louisa, always an enthusiastic reader, enjoyed popular novels of the time, including *Oliver Twist* and *The Vicar of Wakefield*. Abba continued her daughters' sewing lessons, and the girls practiced by making clothes for their dolls.

Learning was never-ending and continued into the

evening hours. After supper, the consociate family gathered at the hearth to hear stories with morals, discuss philosophical questions, and contemplate their weaknesses. These evenings were meant to probe the minds of the community's inhabitants and coax them into a constant state of worthy thought. Questions were asked that required thoughtful answers. The conversations were exhausting for the girls. One night, Louisa wrote, "After a long talk we went to bed very tired." The Fruitlands experience was beginning to take its toll on the Alcott girls.

The Alcotts celebrated Louisa's eleventh birthday (Bronson's forty-fourth) at Fruitlands. On this occasion, Louisa's father asked each family member which fault they most disliked in themselves. Louisa did not need to think long about the question. "I said my bad temper," she wrote that night in her journal.

Weakness and faults were two things the moody Louisa understood well. She battled her strong-willed and fiery personality, hoping to become a gentler person someday. Again and again she sought solace in her journal. Once she wrote, "I felt sad because I have been cross today and did not mind Mother. I cried, and then I felt better." A month later, she vowed to do even better: "I made good resolutions, and felt better in my heart. If I only *kept* all I make, I should be the best girl in the world. But I don't, and so am very bad."

For a time, Louisa's mother was the only woman living at Fruitlands, and all the work of housekeeping fell to her and the girls. While the men wrote articles for *The Dial,* lectured, and recruited new members, Abba and the girls took care of the house and garden. They also brought in the harvest of barley, rye, and wheat at Fruitlands during a season of torrential rainstorms. Lane, Bronson, and the other men were in New York City looking for new recruits. True farmers would not have left such an important task in the hands of children. Much of the harvest was lost.

During the months at Fruitlands, Abba felt that she was sacrificing her daughters' well-being because she had to spend so much of her time and energy taking care of the Lanes and other community members. She longed to leave Fruitlands and resume a happier life elsewhere. In private, after the children were in bed, she told her husband in hushed but angry whispers of her discontent.

By October 8, Abba's birthday, the growing tension in the household was no longer hidden. Lane was urging Bronson to leave his family and join a nearby Shaker community. The two men had visited this religious group and were drawn to its simple ways, prosperous farms, and efficiency of living.

The Shakers—named for the physical shaking of the body during worship—were the most successful religious communal group in the United States. When Bronson and Lane visited the Shaker community near Fruitlands, the Shakers were at the peak of their success, with more than 6,000 members in settlements across

Bronson considered joining the Shakers, a popular religious community named after the shaking of the body during worship.

the eastern United States. Shaker men and women lived separately and did not get married or have children. If Bronson were to join such a community, it would mean the end of the Alcott family.

Louisa and her sisters were terrified that the family would be separated. Louisa wrote in her journal on December 10, "Mr. Lane was in Boston, and we were glad. In the eve father and mother and Anna and I had a long talk. I was very unhappy, and we all cried. Anna and I cried in bed, and I prayed God to keep us all together."

As the difficult New England winter—and mountains of snow—set in, the Fruitlands family was racked with illness. Louisa began suffering from chronic headaches and joint pain that would remain with her the rest of her life. The Alcotts shivered in their flimsy linen clothing and no doubt were undernourished by Lane's sparse diet. Emerson's prediction had come true.

In late December, Abba forced her husband to choose: go by himself with Lane or stay with his family. He chose his family.

In January 1844, Charles and William Lane left Fruitlands for the Shaker community. Shortly afterward, the Alcotts packed their belongings and moved to the nearby community of Still River.

The Fruitlands society had lasted just seven months— until the cold weather, low food and fuel supplies, and frequent quarrels divided the experimental extended family. Louisa later wrote a satirical story called *Transcendental Wild Oats,* which poked fun at the family's Fruitlands experience.

In *Transcendental Wild Oats,* Charles Lane was called Timon Lion, Bronson was Abel Lamb, and Abba was Sister Hope Lamb. In the following excerpt, Timon Lion is instructing the group in the daily schedule. Sister Hope is distressed that Timon himself is doing little work:

"Each member is to perform the work for which experience, strength, and taste best fit for him," continued Dictator Lion. "Thus drudgery and disorder will be avoided and harmony prevail. We shall arise at dawn, begin the day by bathing, followed by music, and then a chaste repast of fruit and bread. Each one finds congenial occupation till the meridian meal; when some deep-searching conversation gives rest to the body and development to the mind. Healthful labor again engages us till the last meal, when we assemble in social communion, prolonged till sunset, when we retire to sweet repose, ready for the next day's activity."

"What part of the work do you incline to yourself?" asked Sister Hope, with a humorous glimmer in her keen eyes.

"I shall wait till it is made clear to me. . . . " responded Brother Timon.

"I thought so." And Mrs. Lamb sighed audibly.

For the time being, with Fruitlands behind her, Louisa was free of threats to what she cherished above all else—her family. She wrote in her journal, "Life is pleasanter than it used to be. . . . Had good dreams, and woke now and then to think, and watch the moon. I had a pleasant time with my mind, for it was happy."

At Hillside, Louisa often retreated to her room for hours to write stories.

Chapter **FOUR**

HILLSIDE

THE FOUR AND A HALF YEARS FOLLOWING THE
Fruitlands experiment were some of the happiest—
and hardest—times Louisa would know. During her
teen years, Louisa began to write with a frantic pace
that she maintained for the rest of her life.

Upon leaving Fruitlands in January 1844, the Alcotts
were nearly penniless. They rented three rooms and
the use of the kitchen in a neighbor's house until they
could afford their own home again. Abba and Bronson visited several communal societies, looking for a
place to live, work, and raise their girls. Still stinging
from Fruitlands, Abba found none suitable for her
and her family.

Bronson, dejected over the failure of Fruitlands,

was suicidal. He tried to starve himself, but Abba forced him to eat. Bronson had often suffered from severe depression, especially following setbacks such as the Temple School and Fruitlands. He experienced dramatic mood swings and believed that he had inherited his mental illness from the Alcott family. Despite his family's needs, Bronson continued to refuse to work for another person. He valued his independence above all else.

The week the family left Fruitlands, Abba received ten dollars (worth about $170 now) from her brother, Sam. She also sold a cloak and a piece of her silver table setting. Fearing for her four daughters, Abba was growing weary of Bronson's refusal to work for a wage. On January 28, 1844, she wrote in her journal, "Should like to see my husband a little more interested in this matter of support."

As Louisa watched her mother carry the burden of providing for the Alcott family, she vowed that someday she would help ease that burden.

The following winter, the family returned to Concord to be near Emerson. Soon after the move, Abba came into a sum of money willed to her by her father, who had died in 1841. With this money and a large donation from Emerson, the Alcotts were able to buy a rambling old house near Emerson's home. They named their new home Hillside.

By this time, Emerson was a well-known and respected writer and lecturer. Magazine editors and book publishers pursued him eagerly. The money he earned from writing and lecturing allowed him to support people he admired, such as Bronson Alcott and poet Ellery Channing. Assisting the Alcotts with the purchase of Hillside helped Emerson fulfill his wish to make Concord an intellectual center.

Located on Lexington Road, Hillside was a colonial structure in a sorry state of disrepair. It was situated

Louisa developed a lifelong passion for nature in the Concord countryside.

on a heavily traveled road, and the traffic annoyed
Bronson. But for Louisa, this new home had every-
thing she loved—a patch of forest for exploring, meadows for running, and a brook for swimming.

Here, Louisa grew from a twelve-year-old girl into a
young woman. At Hillside, Louisa made an important

Bronson sketched his family's Hillside home in 1845.

discovery about herself. One morning she was running in the woods, across the dewy grass, when, she wrote, "A very strange and solemn feeling came over me as I stood there, with no sound but the rustle of the pines, no one near me, and the sun so glorious, as if for me alone. It seemed as if I *felt* God as I never did before, and I prayed in my heart that I might keep that happy sense of nearness all my life." Louisa had discovered God in nature. These two powerful forces would influence her for the rest of her life, and she often turned to nature for comfort and inspiration.

Bronson, who also loved nature, turned his grief over the Fruitlands failure into frantic work. He repaired and enlarged the house and planted melons, cucumbers, beans, potatoes, spinach, beets, rhubarb, and other vegetables. Beyond the house were peach and apple trees and wild grapes. Bronson had hoped to teach in a Concord school, but no one would hire him. Concord residents and school officials still remembered the Temple School scandal of 1836, and they did not believe Bronson was a suitable educator.

For income, the Alcotts continued to depend on loans and donations from friends, small payments from Abba's inheritance, and money from boarders who lived from time to time at Hillside. Bronson also worked odd jobs for Emerson, which contributed some money to the family.

Even at age twelve, Louisa was well aware of her family's reputation in Concord. In a letter to her friend Sophia Gardner in September 1845, Louisa wrote, "Yesterday we went over a little way from our house into some great big fields full of apple-trees, which we climbed, tearing our clothes off our backs (luckily they were old) and breaking our bones, playing tag and all sorts of strange things. We are dreadful wild people here in Concord, we do all the sinful things you can think of."

While the Alcotts could not find a communal society that was right for them, they could form their own. Determined to make a success of communal living, the Alcotts opened Hillside to an orphan boy named Llewellyn Willis, who lived with them for several summers; a teacher, Sophia Foord; and a troubled girl named Eliza Stearns. Eliza's father, a wealthy gentleman, paid Abba to care for his mentally ill daughter.

Louisa did not enjoy the added company at Hillside, especially when the detested Charles Lane returned. Abba hoped that Lane's presence would bring Bronson out of his depression, but Louisa worried that there would not be enough resources for the growing household. "More people coming to live with us; I wish we could be together, and no one else," she wrote in her journal. "I don't see who is to clothe and feed us all, when we are so poor now."

Lane's presence did cheer Bronson, who still shared ideas with his friend, but Louisa turned moodier. One day she called Anna mean and was so ashamed that she "cried over my bad tongue and temper." Another time she wrote, "I am so cross I wish I had never been born." Lane and Sophia Foord took over the girls' schooling. Once again Abba had a houseful of people to care for, as she had at Fruitlands, but Lane no longer held any influence over the family. Abba allowed Lane to stay for a few weeks because he had nowhere else to go. Regardless of how she felt about him, she could not turn away a person in need.

Charles Lane eventually left, and life at Hillside was grand for the Alcott girls, whom Bronson called "a golden band of sisters." They thrived on activity and merriment. The grounds of Hillside became their playground. They made up games like "post office" and "going to Boston," tromped the surrounding woods, and played in the barn on rainy days.

A childhood friend from the neighborhood, Clara Gowing, described Louisa as having "dark brown hair, pleasant grey eyes . . . and a sallow complexion. . . . She was tall and slim . . . and she could walk, run and climb like a boy." Although Louisa and her sisters played with neighborhood children, they were each other's closest friends. Among the neighborhood children, Louisa preferred boys as friends and often wished she were one. She was particularly envious of the freedom boys were given. In the 1800s, a boy's world was larger than a girl's, stretching far beyond the household duties that kept women and girls at home much of the time.

Like the March sisters in *Little Women,* the Alcott girls

loved play acting. Together, Anna and Louisa wrote original dramas with such intriguing titles as "The Witches Curse" and "The Captive of Castile." They also created costumes and scenery and acted the parts, presenting their romances and thrillers in the Hillside attic or in the barn. Lizzie and May acted in small parts, and when Llewellyn Willis was staying with them, he also got a part. "Lords and ladies haunted the garden and mermaids splashed in the bath-house of woven willows over the brook," Louisa wrote about those times. The sisters also delivered monologues and acted famous scenes from literature and fairy tales, including *Jack and the Beanstalk* and *Cinderella.* Louisa, always the leader of the golden band, took charge of the theatrics with full force, organizing the other children as a general might command his soldiers. Clara Gowing described Louisa as a "controlling spirit" who was moody but full of energy and fun.

When the weather was fair, the family joined Emerson and his wife and children on outings. During the summer of 1845, the Alcotts also visited Henry David Thoreau, who was experimenting in "essential living" on nearby Walden Pond. He strived to live off the land in solitude. He later wrote about this experiment in *Walden.* Thoreau played his flute for the Alcott girls, rowed them across Walden Pond, and recounted Native American folklore.

Thoreau and Emerson were romantic figures for the maturing Louisa. She developed schoolgirl crushes on

The Alcott girls spent time on Walden Pond with Thoreau.

them both, though Emerson was in his early forties and Thoreau in his late twenties. She adored Emerson for his mind and Thoreau for his eccentricities and love of nature. Emerson respected Louisa's interest in writing and let her borrow books from his extensive library. She sometimes left wildflowers on Emerson's doorstep and often penned love letters she never delivered.

At Hillside, stories and poems rushed out of Louisa like steam from a whistling teakettle. She wrote fairy

Henry David Thoreau served as an inspirational model for Louisa.

stories and romantic thrillers and conceived the adventurous plays she performed with her sisters.

When Louisa needed to be alone with her thoughts, she stole away to a spot where she could lean up against an old cart wheel that lay half-buried in the ground. Here she dreamed, planned, and wrote. On one visit, she declared to the nearby birds, "I *will* do something by-and-by. Don't care what, teach, sew, act, write, anything to help the family; and I'll be rich and famous and happy before I die, see if I won't!"

The only thing missing from Louisa's life was a room of her own. She longed to read, write, and think in complete solitude. In 1845, she wrote a note to her mother: "I have tryed [sic] to be more contented and I think I have been more so. I have been thinking about my little room which I suppose I shall never have." She signed her note, "from your trying daughter."

The next year, after the many visitors and boarders at Hillside were gone, thirteen-year-old Louisa got her wish. In March 1846, she wrote in her journal, "I have at last got the little room I have wanted so long and am very happy about it. It does me good to be alone, and Mother has made it very pretty and neat for me. My work-basket and desk are by the window, and my closet is full of dried herbs that smell very nice." Her first-floor room had a door that opened onto the garden, so Louisa could run out into the woods whenever she liked.

With her own room, a passion for writing, and a growing sense of responsibility for her family, Louisa made a new resolution. "I have made a plan for my life, as I am in my teens, and no more a child," she wrote in her journal. "I have told no one about my plan, but I'm going to *be* good. . . . Now I'm going to *work really,* for I feel a true desire to improve, and be a help and comfort, not a care and sorrow, to my dear mother." It troubled Louisa to watch helplessly as her mother struggled to provide for her family because her father refused to sacrifice his high ideals.

Abba understood her strong-willed daughter, who each day was growing more and more like her in disposition and outlook. For Louisa's fourteenth birthday, Abba gave her a pen. Abba wrote to Louisa, "Believe me, you are capable of ranking among the best." Bronson gave her a children's book. On the same day, he gave Anna a silver pencil case, gold pen, and gold inkstand; Lizzie two books; and Abba a new rocking chair. One can only imagine the anger and grief that welled up inside Louisa.

When Louisa was fifteen, Emerson asked her to teach his three children. She set up a school in a barn on the Hillside property. She found it difficult to sit still and patiently guide her pupils through their lessons, but she put aside her wishes to be running in the fields, climbing apple trees, or scribbling in her room. To ease her restlessness, she wrote stories about flowers and fairies for her favorite student, eight-year-old Ellen Emerson. At the forefront of Louisa's mind was her plan to provide for her family.

Abba, too, was always thinking about ways to earn money. By the spring of 1848, the Alcotts were again dangerously low on funds. They relied on credit to buy things from Concord shops. With lucky timing, Bronson and Abba were offered jobs at a water therapy spa in Maine. Health spas were popular in the nineteenth century. Sick people came to spas with the hope that water therapies and natural hot springs would cure their illnesses.

Bronson refused to take the job, however, still insisting that he would not work for a wage. Furious, Abba went without him and took the position of matron, leaving her family behind. She worked herself to exhaustion, looking after patients and overseeing meal preparations and housekeeping. After three months, she could no longer bear the separation from her family. She returned to Concord in August.

The Alcotts were able to live for a few months on the money Abba had made. But as winter approached, Abba grew worried. They were again out of money and could not maintain their home. They were so far in debt that Concord shop owners would not give them any additional credit. Bronson's garden, which overflowed with produce in the summer, was not enough to feed them through the winter. There was only one thing left to do. In November 1848—the month Louisa turned sixteen—Abba found a tenant to rent Hillside. The Alcotts moved to Boston, where Abba's relatives had arranged a job for her as a social worker to the city's poor. The family's new home was a cramped apartment.

Louisa was forced to give up her room, her runs in the woods, and the quiet solitude Hillside provided. But a move to Boston could not take from Louisa her most precious possession—her writing ability. That she carried with her wherever she went.

Louisa worked various jobs to ease the family's financial burdens.

Chapter FIVE

THE WRITER

AFTER THE FAMILY MOVED TO BOSTON, THE GIRLS
took turns working at jobs outside the home and taking care of the Alcott household. Although Louisa
would rather have been writing, she accepted the
times when she had to put aside her pen and papers
for a broom and cooking utensils. "I [felt] like a caged
sea-gull as I washed dishes and cooked in the base-
ment kitchen," she wrote years later. While Anna and
Louisa taught school and worked as governesses or
seamstresses, May went to school and developed her
artistic talents. Lizzie, a homebody, probably minded
least when it was her turn to keep house.

Abba was so dedicated to her job as a social worker
that she sometimes gave her poor clients the clothes

she was wearing. But the work was exhausting, and she gave it up for good in April 1850. Later, Abba opened an employment agency for women who wanted to work as maids and in other domestic positions. This work was less grueling and did not take her away from home so much. Bronson held conversations in rooms he rented next door to a bookstore.

Louisa missed the Concord countryside terribly. She wrote in her diary, "Among my hills and woods I had fine free times alone, and though my thoughts were silly, I daresay, they helped to keep me happy and good." She continued to seek quiet times alone, but stolen moments were hard to find in the Alcotts' small Boston apartment and, especially, with so many demands on her time.

During the summers of 1849 and 1850, Louisa found refuge from the family's cramped Boston apartment when the Alcotts were invited to stay in the fashionable Atkinson Street home of Abba's brother, Sam May. Louisa's Uncle Sam had long and patiently supported the family with whatever money he could spare. Like many wealthy city families, during the summer the Mays escaped to a home in the country, where it was cooler. Their city home stood empty until fall.

In the summer of 1849, inspired by her comfortable surroundings, Louisa published a family paper called "The Olive Leaf." She and her sisters filled it with poems, stories, and articles. The following summer on Atkinson Street was very different, however. The entire family contracted smallpox—a highly contagious and deadly disease—from a band of poor children who wandered into the garden looking for food. Bronson's case was the most severe, but everyone survived, nursing each other back to health.

Louisa continued to work toward her goal of supporting her family and easing their chronic financial problems. "Seventeen years have I lived, and yet so little do I know, and so much remains to be done before I begin to be what I desire,—a truly good and useful woman," she wrote in her journal in 1850.

When Louisa was seventeen years old, she wrote her first novel, *The Inheritance.* Surrounded by poverty, Louisa wrote of a wealthy British family who befriended a poor but lovely and talented Italian orphan. The setting was a beautiful English manor. Louisa imagined a world of wealth and beauty far removed from the family's sparse Boston apartment. Unpublished in her lifetime, *The Inheritance* was discovered among Louisa's papers at Harvard University in 1988. The book was published in 1997 and made into a television movie just months later.

Gradually, Louisa grew to love city life. Boston proved inspiring for the budding writer and helped her move closer to achieving her financial goals. In 1850, Louisa earned money from her writing for the first time. She sold her first short story, "The Rival Painters," for $5. A magazine called the *Olive Branch* published it anonymously in May 1852. (A year earlier she had published a poem, "Sunlight," under the pen name Flora Fairfield, in *Peterson's Magazine.*) In 1852, another story called "A Masked Marriage" was published in *Dodge's Literary Museum.* Louisa was paid $10. Louisa recorded all her earnings in her diary.

When Louisa was about eighteen and her family's prospects looked bleak, she visited a barber. How much would he give for her hair, she asked. At five feet, seven inches tall, with sparkling gray eyes, Louisa was an attractive young woman. But she was most proud of her long and luminous chestnut-colored hair, which she considered her best feature. She knew that any barber would be happy to buy it to use for wig-making. Luckily, the Alcotts' situation did not become so bad that she had to make the sacrifice. Years later, Louisa recreated this scene in *Little Women*, when Jo March did sell her hair. Jo used the money for a train ticket to send Marmee to visit the wounded Mr. March.

In 1851, Louisa went to work at a private home in Dedham, Massachusetts. She was employed as a companion to older family members. She was told she would also do light housekeeping tasks, but she ended up doing hard labor, such as lugging water and chopping firewood. She was mistreated by her employers and returned home after she could no longer bear the degrading work.

Just as she had written about her negative experiences at Fruitlands, Louisa penned a tale about her work as a housekeeper. The story "How I Went Out to Service" was published twenty-five years later in the *Independent*. This was the story she offered to publisher James T. Fields—the story he rejected with the curt conclusion that she was no writer.

To shut out the hard times, the Alcott sisters continued to stage plays in their dreary Boston apartment. Anna and Louisa dreamed of becoming professional actresses. For a while, Louisa imagined that she could make more money acting than writing. For Louisa, acting was a joyful, creative outlet that temporarily let her forget that she and her family were "poor as rats & apparently quite forgotten by every one but the Lord."

In the fall of 1852, some good fortune fell upon the Alcotts. The famous author of *The Scarlet Letter*, Nathaniel Hawthorne, purchased Hillside—the home

Anna Alcott

the Alcotts still owned in Concord. The money from the sale allowed the family to move out of the Boston slums and into a small house in a comfortable neighborhood known as Beacon Hill. Here, Anna and Louisa opened another school, and Abba took in boarders.

In her journal's summary for 1852, she wrote, "Father idle, mother at work in the office [Anna] & I governessing, Lizzie in the kitchen, [May] doing nothing but grow. Hard times for all."

In 1853, Bronson lectured to eager audiences in the Midwest, but with little financial gain. In later correspondence with her father, Louisa wrote that she would "prove that though an Alcott *I can* support myself."

For the next four years, Anna and Louisa continued to teach, sew, and look after children, often working away from home and living with their employers. In the summer of 1853, Louisa took a job as a servant, in the home of a relative in Leicester, Massachusetts. This experience was far better than her first domestic job in Dedham.

Although domestic work and sewing took valuable time away from her writing, Louisa knew how much her family needed her wages. And she tried to look at the bright side of the situation: "Sewing won't make my fortune; but I can plan my stories while I work, and then scribble 'em down on Sundays," she reasoned.

Her Sunday scribblings included arranging her fairy stories—written years earlier at Hillside—into a book. Bronson took the manuscript to publisher George W. Briggs, who purchased it. *Flower Fables* was published in December 1854, with 1,600 copies printed in time for Christmas. The stories in *Flower Fables* used fairies, elves, and animals to teach moral lessons, such as patience, duty, and honor. Louisa gave her characters enchanting names such as Thistledown and Lily-Bell. A notice in the *Boston Evening Transcript* advertised the book as "the *most beautiful* Fairy Book that has appeared for a long time . . . by Louisa May Alcott, a young lady of Boston. It will be the most popular juvenile issued this season." The Briggs publishing firm paid Louisa $35 for the book—one dollar more than she had earned working as a servant for four months.

After the book came out, Louisa wrote, "The principal event of the winter is the appearance of my book, 'Flower Fables.' . . . It has sold very well, and people seem to like it. I feel quite proud that the little tales that I wrote for Ellen E[merson] when I was sixteen should now bring money and fame." Although she was pleased with the book, the illustrations disappointed her. She noted that her sister May, already a talented artist at fourteen, could have done better.

When Louisa presented a copy of the book to her mother, she referred to it as her "firstborn." Though just twenty-two, Louisa knew that she would not marry and have a family. She once wrote in her journal, "I'd rather be a free spinster and paddle my own canoe." If she was going to make a living and support her family as a writer, she did not want the additional responsibilities of being a wife and mother. Her books would be her children. That year, Louisa was proud that her earnings allowed her to buy a new bonnet for May and a warm shawl for Abba.

Although Louisa was beginning to succeed as a writer, the Alcotts could not avoid a recurring pattern: money again ran out, and they could no longer afford the rent on their Beacon Hill home. In the summer of 1855, the Alcotts moved to Walpole, New Hampshire, where one of Abba's relatives offered to let the family live rent-free in one of his houses.

Louisa enjoyed being back in the country again. In an 1855 journal entry, she described Walpole as a "lovely place, high among the hills. So glad to run and skip in the woods and up the splendid ravine." As much as she loved the activity and promise of Boston, the countryside refreshed and inspired her. Louisa predicted in her journal, "Shall write here, I know."

The Alcotts were happy in Walpole. They lived in a pretty cottage near relatives. Bronson planted a garden, growing food for the table. Anna and Louisa became

May Alcott at age eighteen

Even though she was hesitant, Louisa, like Jo March in this illustration from Little Women, *knew she had to leave her loving family to make her way in the world.*

involved with a local theatrical group. Louisa wrote in her journal that the days were filled with "plays, picnics, pleasant people, and good neighbors."

As winter set in across the New Hampshire countryside, Louisa grew restless. Her time in the country had refreshed her, but she needed to be back in Boston, where she could sell her stories and earn money. Anna was working as a teacher in Syracuse, New York; Louisa, too, wanted to earn her keep. In November, she wrote in her journal, "Decided to seek my fortune; so, with my little trunk of homemade clothes, $20 earned by stories sent to the "Gazette," and my [manuscripts], I set forth with Mother's blessing one rainy day in the dullest month of the year."

Louisa found 1850s Boston exciting and inspiring.

Chapter SIX

ON HER OWN

IT TOOK COURAGE FOR **LOUISA** TO LEAVE HER FAMILY
and vow to make it on her own in Boston. In the
1850s, it was not considered proper for young women
to live and work without supervision from a trustwor-
thy adult, which usually meant an older male relative.

For much of her life, Louisa felt torn between the
family life she loved but which offered no privacy and
freedom, and the independent city life, which allowed
her the solitude she needed to write. Like working
women before and ever since, Louisa struggled to find
the balance between meeting her own needs and fulfilling those of her family.

In the winter of 1855, Louisa lived with relatives in
Boston. They supplied her with a steady flow of

sewing; she stitched bed linens, men's shirts, women's dresses, and tablecloths. She also found work writing book reviews for magazines. Her cousin, Louisa Willis, was particularly kind to Louisa, giving her gifts of theater and lecture tickets, clothes, and other items Louisa could not afford. Louisa acknowledged in her journal, "I love luxury, but freedom and independence better."

Louisa was glad to be back in the city. "Boston is nicer & noisier than ever. [Street] Cars go rumbling about . . . & crowds of people are swarming up & down in a state of bustle very agreeable to behold after the still life of Walpole," she wrote to her sister Anna, who was teaching at a mental institution in Syracuse, New York.

Louisa's own life was as frantic as the bustling street scenes she described in her letter. She was busy with writing, sewing, trips to the theater and lectures, window-shopping with Cousin Louisa, and visits with friends.

Her stories were being accepted with a regularity that she could depend on. She sent some of the money to her family in Walpole. In January 1856, Louisa was delighted when she noticed "great yellow placards" posted around Boston advertising the publication of "Bertha," her most recent story in the *Saturday Evening Gazette*. People wanted more and more of her writing, and she was only too happy to oblige.

In June, Louisa returned home to find that her sister Lizzie was still suffering the effects of scarlet fever, which she had contracted a year earlier. Louisa spent the summer with the family, nursing Lizzie and sharing in the housekeeping. It was, she wrote, "an anxious time."

In the fall of 1856, before returning to Boston for the winter, Louisa actively sought writing assignments. She wrote to friends, acquaintances, and editors, hoping to find regular, well-paying work. She wrote to William Clapp, the editor of the *Saturday Evening Gazette,* telling him, "I am anxious to know if the popularity of my contributions to the *Gazette* will warrant you to engage with me for a story a month for the coming six at fifteen or twenty dollars each." This was a bold move, since Louisa was asking for a raise. Clapp agreed to buy a story a month, but he continued to pay her only about $10 a story.

As she traveled back to Boston, Louisa prayed to God to "help us all, and keep us for one another." As always, Louisa left her family—and especially Lizzie—reluctantly, but she admitted "There is nothing to do here and there I can support myself and help the family."

In the winter of 1856, Louisa did not live with relatives but instead settled in a boardinghouse where she rented a "sky-parlor" for $3 a week. "I find my little room up in the attic very cosey [sic], and a house full of boarders very amusing to study," she wrote in her journal. Louisa used the boardinghouse experience when she later wrote about Jo March's trip to New York City in *Little Women.*

Like Louisa at the boardinghouse, Jo March finds solitude in the March home attic, as portrayed in Norman Rockwell's 1937 Little Women *illustration.*

Louisa continued sewing and writing at a hectic pace. She also accepted a part-time job teaching Alice Lovering, an invalid girl she had looked after in the past. Louisa even found time to volunteer, teaching in a charity school. Throughout her life, Louisa remembered her parents' belief that no matter how poor the Alcotts were, they were always in a position to help others. "Mother says no one is so poor he can't do a little for some one poorer yet," she wrote in her journal. Volunteering was a sacrifice for Louisa, who did not like teaching and already struggled to squeeze in writing time.

As the year drew to a close, Louisa calculated that she had earned $60 from her stories and $85 from sewing and teaching. In mid-1857, she summed up her success in her journal: "I have done what I planned,—supported myself, written eight stories, taught four months, earned a hundred dollars, and sent money home."

Bronson, too, was at last finding some success. He had been invited to hold conversations in New York City. During his trip, he was asked to lecture about his theories of education at a New Jersey school, and poet Walt Whitman invited Bronson to his home to hold conversations over dinner. Although this round of conversations did not generate much money, Bronson was pleased that people were once again taking an interest in his ideas.

After being away from home, both Bronson and Louisa devoted their energies to the family. In October 1857, the Alcotts moved from Walpole to Concord. Lizzie, never fully recovered from the scarlet fever, was slowly dying. Louisa despaired at the thought of losing her sister: "Find [Lizzie] a shadow, but sweet and patient always. Fit up a nice room for her, and hope home and love and care may keep her."

In the end, the Alcotts' love was not enough to keep

Lizzie with them. She died at the age of twenty-three, early in the spring of 1858.

A part of Louisa never came to terms with the death of her sister. Ten years later, when Louisa wrote *Little Women*, she immortalized Lizzie in the character of gentle Beth March.

Soon after Lizzie's death, the Alcotts moved into a new home in Concord, which Bronson named Orchard House after the property's apple orchard. Louisa nick-named the house "Apple Slump" because the floors

Orchard House, where Louisa wrote Little Women

were uneven. During the first few weeks at Orchard House, Anna, at age twenty-seven, announced her plan to marry John Pratt, the son of a Concord businessman. For Louisa, this meant losing another sister. She confessed to her diary, "I moaned in private over my great loss, and said I'd never forgive J[ohn] for taking Anna from me." Louisa had always been protective of her sisters where suitors were concerned. One boy who had tried to kiss Anna while the family lived at Hillside was given the nickname "Mr. Smack."

For the next few years, Louisa split her time between Boston and Concord, writing, teaching, sewing, and sometimes acting onstage. She probably performed with mixed emotions, since acting must have reminded her of the happy days when the golden band of sisters staged plays at Hillside and in their Boston apartment.

Louisa's writing habits intensified as she grew older. She wrote herself into what she called a "vortex," pouring her thoughts onto the page as if she would burst if she kept them inside. She could work for fourteen hours straight without even pausing for a meal. One biographer wrote of Louisa, "By day and by night she labored as in a daze. She gave little heed to self and little even to her bodily needs."

In her later life, a fan sent Louisa a letter requesting a page of a rough draft of one of her stories or books. She responded, "Dear Sir,—I never copy or 'polish' so I have no old manuscripts to send you." Louisa wrote so intensely that she often produced the final draft in one sitting and without rewriting. She once remarked, "Can't work slowly; the thing possesses me and I must obey till it's done."

In her trancelike writing habits, Louisa was much like her father, who was often so absorbed in his own writing that he, too, neither slept nor ate. But Bronson's intensity sometimes bordered on insanity, while Louisa was able to keep her outside life intact.

Bronson continued to hold conversations in the eastern and midwestern states. He was even invited to speak at Yale University in his home state of Connecticut. Then, in April 1859, Bronson's career took a giant leap forward when he was named superintendent of Concord schools. Bronson was thrilled to be back among students in the profession he loved. Best of all, he was pleased that the people of Concord had finally accepted him. By the late 1850s, as reformers pushed for changes in classroom instruction, Bronson's ideas about nurturing students and making learning fun no longer seemed extreme.

Bronson's success was a great relief to Louisa, who was often the family's only reliable breadwinner. Louisa did not slow down her writing pace, however. During the 1860s, she wrote a number of mystery stories, also known as "blood-and-thunder" tales. They had titles such as "Bath of Blood" and "Abbot's Ghost." Louisa called them "necessity stories" because the money she earned from them paid the bills. She could write these stories quickly, and the pay was better than what she received for her other stories and articles. But she considered these suspenseful tales "rubbish" and published them under a pseudonym, A. M. Barnard. Not even her family knew that A. M. Barnard was really Louisa May Alcott. It wasn't until the 1940s that Louisa was revealed as the author and the stories were published under her real name.

Louisa's necessity stories were serialized in illustrated newspapers. Readers looked forward to each new installment of A. M. Barnard's tales. In 1866, Louisa penned a novel-length blood-and-thunder tale, *A Long and Fatal Love Chase.* Like *The Inheritance,* it was found among her papers at Harvard in 1993. Soon after that, the novel was published and made into a television movie.

By 1860, the United States was on the brink of the Civil War. In the years leading up to the war, politicians across the country debated the issue of slavery and the right of individual states to regulate it. The debates grew more heated as the abolitionist movement gained ground. The abolitionists' opposition to slavery threatened Southerners' way of life. Southern slave owners feared that without slave labor their plantations and crops would not prosper.

The line was finally drawn in 1860, with the election of Abraham Lincoln, a Northerner, to the presidency. Within weeks of Lincoln's election, South Carolina seceded from the Union; other Southern states quickly followed. Deeply held beliefs were put to the test at the point of a bayonet on American battlefields.

When the war began in April 1861, Louisa wished she could march off to battle like the company of soldiers she watched leave Concord. "I long to be a man; but as I can't fight, I will content myself with working for those who can," she remarked.

The Civil War led many men to the battlefields.

After the first major battle of the Civil War, at Manassas, Virginia, thousands of maimed and wounded men flooded into Washington. More followed as the war raged on. Union officials desperately needed trained medical personnel to care for battle-wounded soldiers.

In 1862, Louisa stepped into that role. She learned that a hospital in Washington, D.C., needed nurses to tend wounded soldiers. Louisa knew she had a talent for nursing. She had tended her family with home remedies, had nursed Lizzie before her death, and had cared for little Alice Lovering.

At the age of thirty, Louisa answered the call. She would go to Washington. She was anxious to help the war effort, and she craved a change in her own life. She told her journal, "[I] must let out my pent-up energy in some new way. . . . I want new experiences, and I am sure to get 'em if I go."

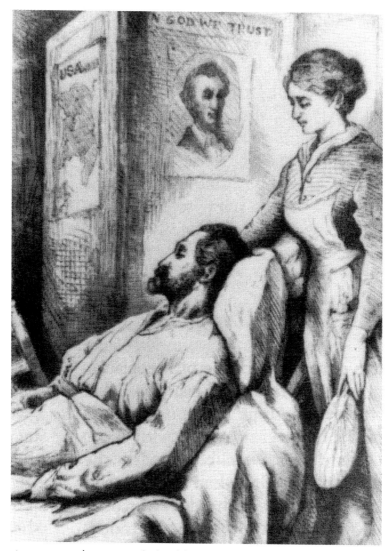

A nurse tends a wounded soldier in an illustration from Hospital Sketches, *a collection of Louisa's wartime stories.*

Chapter **SEVEN**

THE NURSE

APPROACHING HER NEW VENTURE WITH HER USUAL
enthusiasm, Louisa read the works of Florence
Nightingale, the English nurse who began working for
better hospital conditions in 1837. Louisa devoured
Nightingale's *Notes on Nursing,* taking careful notes to
assist her in her own nursing career. She also read
doctors' reports on treating gunshot wounds and other
injuries. If Louisa was going to serve her country, she
would be prepared.

On December 11, 1862, Louisa traveled to Boston,
where she ran errands to prepare for her trip. The
next day, she boarded a train headed for Washington,
D.C. The train rushed south along its tracks, taking
Louisa "into a new world full of stirring sights and

sounds, new adventures, and an evergrowing sense of the great task I had undertaken." Not sure if she would return home dead or alive, she said many prayers during the 500-mile journey.

She arrived at the Union Hotel Hospital—a converted hotel—late in the evening and fell exhausted into a narrow bed in a room she shared with two other nurses. Louisa's first day as a nurse began the next day before the morning light. "Began my new life by seeing a poor man die at dawn, and sitting all day between a boy with pneumonia and a man shot through the lungs," she wrote in her journal.

Just a few days later, soldiers from the Battle of Fredericksburg in nearby Fredericksburg, Virginia, arrived at the hospital. Hundreds of wounded and battered men were packed into the hospital, crowding the corridors and wards. Louisa heard the cries of soldiers having limbs amputated without ether or chloroform to sedate them or any painkiller. While these medicines existed, supplies were often low and doctors were forced to operate without them. As she tended her patients, they recounted the horrible details of battle. She filed these stories away in her mind until she was ready to draw them out in her writing.

Like Florence Nightingale, Louisa was appalled by the conditions she witnessed at the hospital, where soldiers lay "in all stages of suffering, disease & death." The hospital was stifling due to improper ventilation. "No notice is taken of our frequent appeals

Organizations like the Sanitary Commission, pictured here, fought to improve unsanitary conditions in the mid-1800s.

for better ventilation [and] I must do what I can," Louisa wrote.

Improving public and private sanitation was another goal for health reformers in the nineteenth century. Many Americans in the mid-1800s took only sponge baths, washing themselves in a full bath as little as once a year. Unsanitary conditions—including uncollected garbage and horse manure on city streets, polluted drinking water, and unclean outhouses—were commonplace. These conditions attracted insects and rodents, which spread diseases—such as the scarlet fever that had killed Lizzie. Reformers such as Bronson's cousin, William Alcott, instructed Americans in the importance of regular bathing, outdoor exercise, and keeping one's home clean. It wasn't until the Civil War—when thousands of soldiers died from diseases rather than battle wounds—that Americans began to disinfect their homes, businesses, and communities.

In her first weeks at the hospital, Louisa and the other day nurses rose at 6:00 A.M. and dressed by gaslight. One of Louisa's first duties before breakfast was to open the windows to air out the suffocating wards. The hospital was "cold, damp, dirty, full of vile odors from wounds, kitchens, wash rooms, & stables."

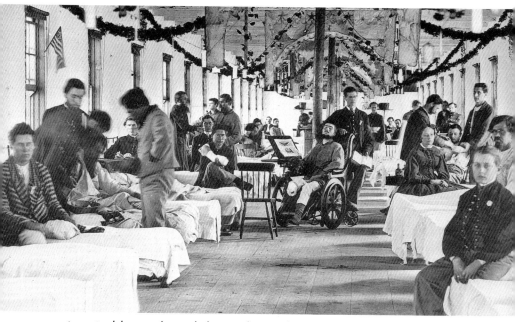

A typical hospital ward during the Civil War

Louisa grew attached to her patients. She was protective of them and once remarked that she wished the doctors would be gentler with her "big babies." The men adored Louisa and enjoyed her mothering. "Find real pleasure in comforting tending & cheering these poor souls who seem to love me," Louisa scribbled in her journal during a spare moment.

After her breakfast, Louisa fed and washed "her boys," made beds and swept the floor, emptied bedpans, and assisted the doctors with changing bandages and locating linens, sponges, and other supplies. In the afternoon, Louisa visited with the soldiers, read them newspapers, told stories, and did what she could to make them comfortable. She sometimes helped them write letters home. At times she had to deliver to loved ones the sad news that a soldier had died. "The answering of letters from friends after some one has died is the saddest & hardest duty a nurse has to do," she wrote in her journal.

Louisa sometimes worked the night shift, from noon to midnight. She enjoyed this change of schedule. It gave her free time during the day to go exploring and have her morning runs, which she believed would keep her healthy. On one outing, Louisa strolled past the White House and caught a glimpse of President Abraham Lincoln as he rode along the street on a gray horse. Louisa entertained the soldiers with lively details of her outings.

Constantly on call for doctors and patients, Louisa

once joked in her journal that she would trade all her possessions for fifteen minutes of rest. Like so many nurses, Louisa suffered from overwork and poor working conditions. She wrote in her journal in early January 1863, "Bad air, food, water, work & watching are getting to be too much for me."

After only three weeks on the job, Louisa developed a painful cough. By mid-January, she had a severe case of deadly typhoid pneumonia. Louisa was ordered to bed. For days she tossed and turned, feverish and delirious. The doctors gave her large doses of calomel, a strong medicine, in hopes of purging her body of the fever.

The hospital matrons took action when it was clear that Louisa was gravely ill. They sent a telegram to Bronson, who came immediately to take his sick daughter home. At first, Louisa was angry with him. She preferred to be nursed back to health at the hospital, hoping she would improve and could continue working. But within a week after Bronson's arrival, he took Louisa home to Orchard House and her family. Louisa's nursing career was over.

For weeks at home, Louisa drifted in and out of feverish delusions. She barely knew her family. She could not eat, and her body grew thin and wasted. Her long and beautiful hair, difficult to care for and uncomfortable for Louisa, had to be cut away. She was near death. Emerson's wife sent a maid to Orchard House to help Abba with the household chores, so Abba could spend more time by her daughter's side. As Bronson, Abba, and May nursed Louisa, they must have relived the painful ordeal of Lizzie's death five years earlier.

Anna was now living with her husband in Boston. She was seven months pregnant and was discouraged from visiting her sister. Bronson wrote Anna frequently to update her on Louisa's progress. He did not reveal the seriousness of her case.

Louisa recuperated from typhoid pneumonia in her room at Orchard House.

Louisa's fever eventually passed, but Louisa was not yet well. "Found a queer, thin, big-eyed face when I looked in the glass, didn't know myself at all & when I tried to walk discovered that I couldn't, & I cried because my legs wouldn't go," she wrote. Louisa faced many weeks of slow recovery as she taught herself to walk again. Not until March was she sitting up in bed, walking around a little, and eating regularly.

Good news arrived on March 28—Anna had given birth to a healthy baby boy. By April, Louisa was back to her old self. She was enjoying walks, sewing a little, and thinking about what to do next.

The answer came in the suggestion of a publisher friend who convinced her to publish the letters she had written home from the Union Hotel Hospital. The Civil War still raged, and the American public was hungry for news of battles and soldiers. Louisa's "Hospital Sketches" were serialized in *The Commonwealth*, a Boston periodical. Louisa wrote dramatic passages about what she saw and did in the hospital:

> The sight of several stretchers, each with its legless, armless, or desperately wounded occupant, entering my ward, admonished me that I was there to work, not to wonder or weep; so I corked up my feelings, and returned to the path of duty, which was rather a 'hard road to travel' just then. . . . Forty beds were prepared, many already tenanted by tired men who fell down anywhere,

and drowsed till the smell of food roused them.
Round the great stove was gathered the dreariest
group I ever saw—gaunt and pale, mud to the
knees, with bloody bandages untouched since put
on days before; many bundled up in blankets,
coats being lost or useless.

The sketches proved so popular that Louisa quickly
wrote more. Soon, two publishers were asking Louisa
to sell them the book rights to the material. Her second book, *Hospital Sketches,* was published in August
1863 under the pen name of Tribulation Periwinkle.
Louisa was pleased that her publisher, James Redpath,
agreed to donate a percentage of his profits to benefit
war orphans.

During the summer of 1863, Louisa was selling stories as fast as she could write them. Publishers of
such prominent periodicals as *The Atlantic* sought
more work by the popular author of *Hospital Sketches.*
They were even asking for more books.

With the money from *Hospital Sketches,* $10 from
nursing, and prize money from a contest she had won
the previous January, Louisa redecorated a room in
Orchard House that would be her own place to think
and work. She bought new furniture, and May helped
her with the wallpapering and painting.

Although Louisa was finally achieving her lifelong
dreams, she was still somewhat surprised by the attention she was getting. She confessed in her journal,

"A year ago I had no publisher & went begging with my wares; now *three* have asked me for something. . . . Fifteen years of hard grubbing may be coming to something after all."

Louisa had bounced back from her illness to become a popular author courted by prominent Boston publishers. But the typhoid fever had left its mark. Calomel, the drug she was given at the hospital, contained high levels of mercury, which is poisonous. For the rest of her life, Louisa suffered from the effects of mercury poisoning. She would never be as strong as she once had been, and she was seldom free of flus, coughs, severe headaches, fatigue, and other chronic ailments. But she would not stop writing.

During the next few years, life was more comfortable for the Alcotts. Louisa continued to write and publish numerous stories. She resurrected an old manuscript called *Moods* and set to work finishing it. The romantic novel was published in 1864. Soon, life returned to normal for the nation as well: the Civil War ended in April 1865.

Later that same year, Louisa fulfilled a dream of traveling to Europe. She was hired as a traveling companion for Anna Weld, a young invalid, and her brother, George. The group traveled first to England, where Louisa strolled through parks and toured Westminster Abbey. Louisa was not thrilled with the cold, damp English climate and was glad when they left for Belgium and Germany, where Anna received medical treatment. In Germany, Louisa saw the Alps and enjoyed a boat trip on the Rhine River. She spent her days reading, writing, walking, taking French lessons, and fulfilling her obligations as a companion to Anna. Louisa was sometimes homesick, but letters from home and American newspapers helped. From Germany, the group traveled to Italy and France.

Before returning to Concord, Louisa was able to spend a few weeks traveling by herself; she was growing weary of the constant company of other people. She traveled to Paris and then back to England, where she attended the theater and a lecture by author Charles Dickens. Her final task before sailing for home was to arrange for a British edition of her novel *Moods,* which was published in England in August 1866.

Back home in the United States, *Moods* was selling with limited success. Some book reviewers thought she could do better, including the esteemed author Henry James, who wrote in 1865, "There is no reason why Miss Alcott should not write a very good novel.... When such a novel comes, as we doubt not it eventually will, we shall be among the first to celebrate it."

May Alcott drew the frontispiece for the first edition of Little Women.

Chapter **EIGHT**

LITTLE WOMEN

IN **SEPTEMBER 1867, THOMAS NILES, ONE OF**
Louisa's publishers, suggested that she write a book
for girls. At the same time, another publisher, Horace
Fuller, asked her to be the editor of a popular children's magazine, *Merry's Museum*. As editor, Louisa
would read and edit manuscripts and write one story
and one editorial per month. "Said I'd try," she wrote
unenthusiastically in her journal. "Began at once on
both new jobs, but didn't like either."

Louisa did not want to write for girls; she would
rather have tried a novel for boys. Her primary reason
for taking on both assignments was money. The job at
Merry's Museum paid $500 a year, and she thought her
girls' story might bring in a few hundred more.

In October, Louisa left Concord for Boston. She needed a quiet place to work if she were to fulfill her new obligations. She loaded up her furniture from Orchard House and moved into a rented room she nicknamed "Gamp's Garret" after a character in a Charles Dickens novel. Her new home was conveniently located near the offices of several prominent Boston publishers. As always, the independence renewed Louisa's spirit. "I am in my little room," she wrote contentedly, "spending busy, happy days, because I have quiet, freedom, work enough, and strength to do it."

During these months in Boston, Louisa worked on *Merry's Museum* and wrote stories for publishers eager for her work. She continued to be amazed by her success. In January 1868, she wrote to her mother, "I often think as I am going around, independent, with more work than I can do, & half a dozen publishers asking for tales, of the old times when I went meekly from door to door peddling my first poor little stories." She recognized that she was no longer a beginner, but an established professional with a hard-earned reputation.

Despite her busy schedule, Louisa found time to act in charity plays around the Boston area. The plays disrupted her writing time, but she continued anyway "because I have no money to give." Although her income continued to increase—she expected to make $1,000 in 1868 from her writing—Louisa did not have much money left over after paying her bills, helping

Louisa's job at Merry's Museum, a popular nineteenth-century children's magazine, provided her with a steady income.

May get established as an art teacher in Boston, and sending money home to her parents in Concord. These letters came with cheery but cautious instructions: "Keep all the money I send; pay up every bill, get comforts & enjoy yourselves. Let's be merry while we may. And lay up a bit for a rainy day."

Louisa's work at the magazine was taking up more time than she expected, and she found herself doing more than she had agreed to do. "Fuller [her publisher] seems to expect me to write the whole magazine, which I did not bargain for," she complained in

January 1868. By February, Louisa had not done much work on the girls' story she had been asked to write months earlier. Her time away from the magazine was devoted to attending lectures, the theater, and the annual meeting of the Massachusetts Anti-Slavery Society.

At the end of February, Louisa was called home to care for Abba, who was ill. Even as a middle-aged woman, Louisa continued to feel the pull between her family in Concord and an independent life in Boston. "I am sorry to leave my quiet room," she wrote, "for I've enjoyed it very much." At the same time, she was pleased that she could make her mother comfortable. "Had the pleasure of providing Marmee with many comforts, and keeping the hounds of care and debt from worrying her," she wrote. "She sits at rest in her sunny room, and that is better than any amount of fame to me."

In May, Thomas Niles asked Louisa about the story for girls. Louisa admitted in her journal, "Lively, simple books are very much needed for girls, and perhaps I can supply the need." She resolved to try again.

She decided her main characters, the four March girls, would be modeled after herself and her sisters. But before writing a story based on her family, Louisa shared her ideas with them. "Marmee, Anna, and May all approve my plan," she wrote in May 1868. And so she picked up her pen and started what was to become her most famous work. "I plod away, though I don't enjoy this sort of thing. Never liked girls or knew many, except my sisters; but our queer plays and experiences may prove interesting, though I doubt it."

Sitting in her room in Orchard House, Louisa let her childhood memories flow from her pen. Louisa herself was Jo March in the story. Jo was impetuous and passionate, "very tall, thin, and brown, and reminded one of a colt." Jo had a dreadful temper, much like Louisa's own. "I am Jo March," Louisa once said.

Anna was the beautiful Meg March. The eldest sister, Meg tried her best to bear poverty, although she would have preferred a more comfortable life.

Louisa immortalized Lizzie in the angel-like Beth March, described as "a housewifely little creature [who] helped Hannah keep home neat and comfortable for the workers, never thinking of any reward but to be loved." Beth and the rough-and-tumble Jo were soulmates in the book, as Louisa and Lizzie had been in real life.

Artistic Amy March was nicknamed the "Little Raphael," Louisa's fond name for May.

Drawing on boys she had known in her youth, Louisa created the character of Laurie Laurence, the lonely neighbor boy who befriends the March sisters and falls in love with Jo. Laurie's kindly uncle, Mr. Laurence, was modeled after Louisa's own Uncle Sam.

Louisa set the story in New England during the Civil War, a time she had found invigorating and adventurous. She modeled the old and rambling March home

after Hillside—where the golden band of sisters had
been the happiest. Louisa had once described Hillside
as the "golden age of the Alcotts." Inspired as well by
her current surroundings, Louisa added a few charac-
teristics from Orchard House. She modeled the home
of Meg March after Dove Cottage in Concord.

The four March sisters staged plays, dreaming up

*Louisa and Lizzie were close companions, much like Jo and Beth
in this illustration from* Little Women.

villains and heroines and exotic costumes and sets, just as the Alcott sisters had done. The Marches also published a family newspaper, as Louisa had during her teenage years in Boston. In the book, the four girls decide to form a secret literary society, named after Charles Dickens's novel *The Pickwick Papers*. The Marches' club was called the Pickwick Club.

> They . . . met every Saturday evening in the big garret, on which occasion the ceremonies were as follows: Three chairs were arranged in a row before a table on which was a lamp, also four white badges with a big 'P.C.' in different colors on each, and the weekly newspaper called *The Pickwick Portfolio*, to which all contributed something, while Jo, who reveled in pens and ink, was the editor. At seven o'clock, the four members ascended to the clubroom, tied their badges round their heads, and took seats with great solemnity. . . . Pickwick [Meg], the president, read the paper, which was filled with original tales, poetry, local news, funny advertisements, and hints, in which they good-naturedly reminded each other of their faults and shortcomings.

Because her work was fiction, and only loosely based on fact, Louisa could improve upon real life. Rather than expose her father's shortcomings and inability to support his family, Louisa created an absent

In Little Women, *Louisa created an ideal father who was away at war, unlike Bronson Alcott. "Marmee" and her four daughters were closely united by love and friendship.*

father in Mr. March. By sending him off to be a chaplain in the war, she gave him a noble profession. In Mrs. March, Louisa created a strong and loving mother who bore hard times without the frustration and anger that had plagued Abba. Louisa gave this character the loving nickname she had for her own mother, "Marmee."

Like the Alcotts, the Marches were poor, and the two oldest daughters helped support the family. "When Mr. March lost his property in trying to help an unfortunate friend, the two oldest girls begged to be allowed to do something toward their own support," Louisa wrote in *Little Women*. Meg became a governess, as Anna had done, and Jo was a companion to the unbearable Aunt March.

Interspersed in the book were Bronson's theories, principles, and ideas for reform, which people had scorned throughout much of his life. The March girls received an unusual education, and though they were religious, they did not attend church. They shared their meager resources with those who had less than they did, just as Bronson Alcott had shared the family's firewood so many years before. At the beginning of *Little Women*, Marmee asks the girls to give their Christmas breakfast feast—their only present—to a poor neighbor family.

"Merry Christmas, little daughters! . . . I want to say one word before we sit down. Not far away from here lies a poor woman with a little newborn baby. Six children are huddled into one bed to keep from freezing, for they have no fire. There is nothing to eat over there, and the oldest boy came to tell me they were suffering hunger and cold. My girls, will you give them your breakfast as a Christmas present?"

They were all unusually hungry, having waited nearly an hour, and for a minute, no one spoke— only a minute, for Jo exclaimed impetuously, "I'm so glad you came before we began!"

"May I go and help carry the things to the poor little children?" asked Beth eagerly.

"*I* shall take the cream and the muffins," added Amy, heroically giving up the articles she most liked.

Meg was already covering the buckwheats, and piling the bread into one big plate.

"I thought you'd do it," said Mrs. March, smiling as if satisfied. "You shall go and help me, and when we come back we will have bread and milk for breakfast, and make it up at dinnertime."

Louisa also incorporated the Alcotts' abolitionist stance into *Little Women*. The March girls did not wear clothes produced from cotton grown in the South. For Louisa, this idea dated back almost twenty-five years, when she and her family had worn linen tunics at Fruitlands.

Louisa wrote the first part of *Little Women* in less than three months, returning to her exhausting yet familiar vortex. By the end of her writing frenzy, she was "very tired, head full of pain from overwork."

Both Louisa and Thomas Niles were disappointed with the manuscript. But when Niles passed it on to his niece to read, she pronounced it "splendid" and asked for more. He knew he was about to publish something special.

Now that the book had been accepted, only contract negotiations remained. Niles offered two options:

With the publication of Little Women, *thirty-six-year-old Louisa* became a world-famous author.

Louisa could sell all rights to the book for $1,000, or she could accept $300 in advance plus royalties (payments based on future sales). Thomas Niles advised her to take the latter, even though it might mean less profit for his firm. Louisa took his advice.

When the page proofs arrived in August, Louisa's perception of the book changed. "It reads better than I expected," she admitted. "Not a bit sensational, but simple and true, for we really lived most of it." She asked May to illustrate the book.

When *Little Women* appeared in September 1868, it sold out in only a month. As more and more people clamored for copies, additional books were printed and publishing firms in other countries scrambled for the right to print it in foreign languages. Within three years, 87,000 copies of *Little Women* had been sold. Louisa had found her golden egg.

Louisa was glad she had not sold the book outright. If she had, she and her heirs would not have received payments from future sales. *Little Women* brought in thousands of dollars each year and ensured that she and her family would never again experience the hardships of poverty. At the age of thirty-six, Louisa had finally accomplished her goal to bring lasting comfort and security to her family.

Most critics in the United States and later in England and other countries praised *Little Women*. One reviewer wrote that the book "took hold of young minds, especially the minds of girls." Another described it as "lively" and "exceedingly interesting." Some critics thought the novel was too mature for children but applauded it nonetheless.

Little Women appealed to many readers simply because it was a realistic story about ordinary girls. Many books of the time portrayed young heroines in dramatic but unrealistic situations. And with the shadow of the Civil War only three years behind them, Americans welcomed a story that made them feel good about the world. Families welcomed the Marches into their homes as if reuniting with dear friends.

Many families read and reread the book. As far away as the Midwestern prairies, the Mathers, an Iowa farm family, often reread the story of the Marches of New

England. The Mather girls pretended they were the March sisters, acting out scenes from the book. One of the Mather sisters later wrote in her memoirs, "Rachel was Meg, Edith Jo, Jeannette Amy. Paul was welcomed as Laurie. When another sister arrived she was acclaimed as Beth on sight.... Now our cast was complete and our dramatization of *Little Women* was no longer handicapped by shortage in main characters."

By November 1868, Louisa was back in Boston. Abba was snug in Anna's home for the winter, and Bronson was lecturing in the Midwest. Louisa settled into a room on Brookline Street and resumed work on *Merry's Museum*. She also began a sequel to *Little Women* called *Good Wives*. (Since 1920 the two books have been published as one under the title *Little Women*.) The sequel would provide answers to fan mail from girls around the country who wanted to know how the story ended and who the March girls married. Some of these letters disturbed Louisa. She was upset that her readers believed that marriage was "the only end and aim of a woman's life." Louisa had hoped that *Little Women* would inspire girls towards independence, not dependence on husbands, brothers, and fathers.

Specifically, Louisa's fans wanted Jo to marry Laurie. But Louisa stood firm. She wrote in her journal: "I *won't* marry Jo to Laurie to please any one." After years of struggling to achieve success, Louisa May Alcott wasn't about to sacrifice her ideals to suit the wishes of her fans.

Louisa's ability to write realistic stories and characters earned
her the title, "The Children's Friend."

Chapter **NINE**

THE CHILDREN'S FRIEND

THE NEXT TWENTY YEARS BROUGHT SUCCESS, SORROW, and sickness to the famous Miss Alcott. Although she had accomplished her life's goal, she had paid a high price, and she knew it. She had settled the Alcotts' debts and made her family secure. But she continued to be plagued with ill health. "My headaches, cough, and weariness keep me from working as I once could, fourteen hours a day," she wrote in her journal.

Three months after she had delivered the *Good Wives* manuscript, Louisa admitted that she felt "quite used up." Her publisher, Roberts Brothers, was asking for a new book, but Louisa did not want to put her health at risk. "I am afraid to go into a vortex lest I fall ill," she remarked.

To make matters worse, her fame brought a steady stream of reporters and curious fans to Orchard House. Admirers sketched her likeness as she picked pears in the orchard. Reporters hung about and scribbled furiously in their notebooks. And some people even ventured to talk to Louisa's two young nephews, Frederick and John Pratt. Sometimes, without first consulting Louisa, Bronson invited guests to Orchard House to meet his famous daughter. Louisa disliked the attention because it interfered with her work. "People *must* learn that authors have some rights," she wrote hotly in her journal. "I can't entertain a dozen a day and write the tales they demand also."

In addition to supporting the Alcotts financially, Louisa's fame helped to rekindle interest in Bronson and his ideas. His life's work, *Tablets,* a collection of philosophical essays and poems, had been published by Louisa's publisher shortly after *Little Women* came out. Louisa's success helped Bronson in other ways, too. Her earnings equipped him for his lecture tours in the Midwest. "Got Father off for the West, all neat and comfortable," she wrote after a shopping spree. "I enjoyed every penny spent, have had a happy time packing his new trunk with warm flannels, neat shirts, gloves, etc., and seeing the dear man go off in a new suit, overcoat, hat . . . like a gentleman." No longer did people laugh at Bronson Alcott. Wherever he traveled he was welcomed as the father of *Little Women.* Crowds begged him for news of his famous daughter.

Always the charmer and a dynamic orator, Bronson entertained Louisa's fans with stories of her unusual and adventurous life.

In 1879, Bronson opened a school of philosophy in a building constructed on the Orchard House property. Men and women from across the country descended on Concord to discuss philosophical questions with Bronson. Although Louisa was pleased about her father's success, his visitors—like the reporters and fans who came to see her—were a constant source of distraction. The presence of the philosophers also struck at the core of Louisa's personality. She was a doer, while Bronson was a thinker. It was frustrating for

Bronson Alcott poses in the doorway of his school of philosophy at Orchard House.

Louisa to watch people talk about the world's problems instead of solving them. "Why discuss the Unknowable till our poor are fed & the wicked saved?" she wondered soon after Bronson's school opened.

In a roundabout way, the unreliable and stubborn Bronson was partly responsible for his daughter's success. His ideas for societal reforms fueled Louisa's imagination and steered her pen. His positions on education and women's independence found their way into Louisa's life and writing. Throughout his life, Bronson had argued that there should be better and more realistic books for children to enjoy. Who better to write them than his own daughter?

When Louisa wasn't writing and looking after her family, she worked for the causes she believed in and had grown up defending. She continued her charity work, sharing her time and talents with orphans, the poor, and prisoners. She organized a temperance society in objection to what she described as "a great deal of drinking" in Concord, and a suffrage society to work towards women's right to vote. She had little patience for people who didn't agree with her ideals. "So hard to move people out of the old ruts," she wrote. "I haven't patience enough. If they wont [sic] see . . . I let em alone & steam along my own way."

Very outspoken about her ideas, Louisa wrote and published letters to the editor in several publications, including the new *Woman's Journal*. She sometimes signed her letters "Yours for reform." Louisa was asked to write the introduction to a book about the women's suffrage movement, but she refused, noting in a letter to her publisher, "I don't write prefaces well." As passionately as she felt about the subject, she would have preferred to write the book itself rather than just its introduction. In 1879, when women were given the right to vote in Concord elections, Louisa was the first woman in town to register. Later, she donated money to help start a health center run by two female doctors. Louisa knew firsthand how difficult it was for women to establish themselves in careers reserved for men.

Between 1870 and 1888, Louisa divided her time between Concord and Boston, with vacations in Canada and Maine. She and May traveled to Europe in 1870 and spent many months in Rome, where May studied art. Louisa returned home in June 1871, leaving May to pursue her artistic studies in Europe.

During the last eighteen years of her life, Louisa wrote and published twenty-seven books—mostly for children—including *Eight Cousins, Rose in Bloom,* and *Under the Lilacs.* She also wrote countless magazine articles and stories. Most of her children's books are still in print. Louisa also contributed regularly to the most popular children's magazines of the time, including *The Youth's Companion* and *St. Nicholas,* as well as prominent adult periodicals.

These magazines no longer paid her $5 or $10 a story. Louisa demanded—and received—hundreds and sometimes thousands of dollars for works she sold to periodicals. Her children's books were also selling better than she ever dreamed. *An Old-Fashioned Girl,* for example, sold 12,000 copies in advance and 27,000 copies within one month of its publication in 1870. Each year, Louisa's publishers reprinted thousands of copies of her novels. Louisa was earning thousands of dollars a year—more than enough to support her family comfortably, with funds left over to invest for the future. Louisa continued to record her earnings in her journal and had also begun a new section to record her investments.

This success came partly because Louisa lived and wrote during a revolutionary time in the publishing and printing industries. By the 1860s, new printing inventions made it possible to mass-produce inexpensive newspapers, magazines, and books. By the 1870s, almost anyone—even the poorest Americans—could afford to buy reading materials. At the same time, literacy rates had increased, and more and more Americans wanted to read for pleasure.

Although Louisa preferred writing for adults, she continued to write for children because her stories were so popular and profitable. Fame and financial security, however, allowed Louisa to choose her themes. She poked fun at society and advocated education reform, labor reform, and women's rights. In *Little Men* and *Eight Cousins* she put forth some of Bronson's radical ideas for improvements in education. *Silver*

Pitchers tackled temperance, and *Work* pushed for women's independence and right to vote.

Published in 1873, *Work* was another autobiographical novel. Through the character of Christie, a young woman who wished to be independent, Louisa profiled the numerous jobs she had held throughout her life, including actress, servant, and seamstress. The story opens with Christie telling her aunt why she wants to try life on her own:

> I'm old enough to take care of myself; and if I'd been a boy, I should have been told to do it long ago. I had to be dependent; and now there's no need of it, I can't bear it any longer. . . . Let me go Auntie and find my place wherever it is.

Louisa dedicated this novel to Abba, writing, "To my mother, whose life has been a long labor of love, this book is gratefully inscribed by her daughter." Abba's prediction twenty-seven years earlier that her daughter was "capable of ranking among the best" had come true.

Louisa's most successful years also brought great sadness, with the deaths of four family members.

Her brother-in-law, John Pratt, passed away in 1870. Louisa instinctively took on the role of provider for her widowed sister and fatherless nephews. "Began to write a new book, 'Little Men,' that John's death may not leave A[nna] and the dear boys in want," Louisa

From left to right: *Louisa, Abba, Anna's child Freddy, Anna, and Bronson at Orchard House in the early 1870s*

wrote soon after John's death. When *Little Men* was published at the end of June 1871, 50,000 copies had already been ordered in advance.

Throughout the rest of her life, Louisa provided for her nephews as if they were her own children. Although she had once resented John Pratt for taking Anna out of the Alcott nest, Louisa had come to love him as a brother and genuinely grieved his death.

Soon after John's death, Uncle Sam May died. He had been the family's faithful provider from the time Louisa was a girl. "Dear Uncle S. J. May died; our best friend for years," Louisa wrote sadly in her journal. "He leaves a sweeter memory behind him than any man I know." In a way, Louisa's Uncle Sam had been the financial provider that Bronson never was.

Louisa's mother died in 1877, and Louisa missed her terribly. She longed to write a tribute to her mother expressing all that Marmee had meant to her, but she never found the words. "Began a memoir of Marmee," she wrote in her journal, "but had to give it up." The memories were just too painful. Years later, Louisa carried out her mother's wishes and destroyed many of Abba's personal papers, including diaries she had kept as a child.

The following year, some welcome news arrived from Louisa's sister May. She joyfully told her family of her marriage to Ernest Nieriker, a Swiss businessman she had met while traveling in Europe in the late 1870s. May and Ernest lived in Paris, where May was studying art. Ernest was a great comfort to May while she mourned Abba's death. Within a year, May gave birth to a daughter, Louisa May Nieriker.

Tragically, just seven weeks after the birth, May died from meningitis. In her will, May left instructions that she wanted her child to be raised by her namesake, Louisa May Alcott of Boston and Concord. The child's father was crushed by his wife's death and moved to

Baden, Germany, shortly afterwards. Louisa wrote in her journal that he had agreed to the custodial arrangement because he wanted to respect May's wish that Louisa raise the child.

Suddenly, forty-eight-year-old Louisa was a mother. In the autumn of 1880, Louisa went to the Boston wharf to greet her new ward. A ship captain carried Lulu, as the toddler was called, off the boat and into Louisa's arms. Lulu called her "Marmar."

Lulu brought much happiness into Louisa's life, but Louisa found it hard to keep up with an energetic toddler. Lulu often stayed in Anna's home in Concord, where she had cousins to entertain her.

As the years went by, Louisa's illnesses worsened. At times, her throat was so sore and hoarse that she could not speak. Rheumatoid arthritis inflamed her joints and she had trouble walking. Sometimes she found it difficult to digest food. Louisa took morphine to help with her pain. In the nineteenth century, doctors often prescribed morphine for pain, not knowing it was an addictive drug. Some historians think that Louisa suffered from cancer in addition to arthritis and mercury poisoning. In the last three years of her life, Louisa found it increasingly difficult to make full entries in her journal. She wrote quick, abbreviated observations about her health, the family, and her activities. At times, her doctor, Rhoda Lawrence, forbade her to write.

Bronson, too, was ailing. In 1882 he had a stroke

Always devoted to her family, Louisa cared for her niece Lulu after May's death.

and was unable to continue his philosophical discussions. Louisa sold Orchard House and moved her family to Boston. She rented a house in one of Boston's finest neighborhoods, far away from the slums and poverty she had once experienced.

Despite Bronson's inability to express his affection and admiration for Louisa, he loved his daughter very much. And he understood, perhaps better than anyone except Abba, the power of Louisa's intense personality. In a letter to his wife, he had once referred to Louisa as an "arsenal." On the first day of March in 1888, as Bronson lay dying, he beckoned to Louisa, "Come with me." When she left his side, knowing that her father would live only a few more days, Louisa herself became gravely ill. She drifted in and out of consciousness for the next five days. On March 6, 1888, at the age of fifty-five, Louisa May Alcott died

Louisa was buried among her mentors, Ralph Waldo Emerson and Henry David Thoreau.

from pneumonia and other illnesses. She had been too sick for Anna to tell her that her father had already died, three days earlier.

Louisa was buried on "Author's Ridge" in Concord's Sleepy Hollow Cemetery, not far from the resting places of her friends Ralph Waldo Emerson and Henry David Thoreau. At the funeral, Louisa's friend Ednah Cheney read a poem written by Bronson in which he referred to his daughter as "duty's faithful child." The reading honored Louisa's lifelong dedication to her family. Louisa's name had come to signify "exalted worth," as her father had hoped at her birth.

Sometime before her death, Louisa destroyed many of her letters and diary entries, particularly those she believed to be too personal. Just as Abba had not wanted strangers poking through her papers, Louisa wanted to keep part of her life private. She did not destroy all of her papers, however, and her first biographer—her friend and fan Ednah Cheney—was able to draw on what remained to tell the story of the famous American author who became known as "The Children's Friend."

EPILOGUE

Louisa's fans around the world mourned her death. Literary critics wrote that Louisa's death at such a young age deprived her readers of more books in the fine tradition of *Little Women*.

Ednah Cheney's biography of Louisa May Alcott, published in 1888, was followed by many published remembrances of the famous author. People who had known Louisa—if only for a few years in childhood—wrote books and magazine articles about her. Clara Gowing, who had known the Alcott girls in Concord in the 1840s, published *The Alcotts as I Knew Them in 1909*. Clara wrote about playing with Louisa and her sisters near a swampy patch of land they called "Paradise" and about the post office game Louisa created for their amusement.

Julian Hawthorne, son of author Nathaniel Hawthorne and a neighbor of the Alcotts, also recalled his lifelong relationship with Louisa. In 1922, he published a tribute to Louisa in *Ladies' Home Journal*. He remembered being invited to "Apple Slump" for lively evenings filled with laughter and dramatics.

Louisa's fans devoured these tributes. Time has not lessened the public's interest in the author of *Little Women*. Her best-known novel influenced juvenile literature, as authors who came after her continued to create realistic settings and characters.

Little Women was dramatized on stages throughout the United States and in Europe. Fans loved to see the Marches come to life. Just thirty years after her death and twenty-five years after the invention of motion pictures, Louisa's masterpiece novel was made into a movie. The first film of *Little Women* was a silent version directed and produced by William A. Brady and Harley Knowles, two distinguished figures of the early 1900s. For a few hours, movie and theatergoers were transported to 1860s New England and shared in the joys and sorrows of the four March sisters. In later years, *Little Women* was made into television movies and other silver-screen versions. In 1933, actress Katharine Hepburn tackled the role of Jo March to much acclaim.

Most recently, well-known actresses Winona Ryder, Susan Sarandon, and Claire Danes stepped into the roles of Jo, Marmee, and Beth March in a 1994 version of *Little Women* directed by Gillian Armstrong. The movie was a huge success when it was released, earning record profits at the box office. Accompanying the film's release was a companion novelization of the movie written by well-known children's author Laurie Lawlor. This version of *Little Women* sold more than 300,000 copies in just months.

This book also caused some controversy, however. Louisa's original book is almost 500 pages and written in flowery Victorian language. Lawlor's book is a simplified version of *Little Women* that runs about a third the length of the original. Some educators believed that young people would miss out on the real experience if they read Lawlor's version instead of the original.

But controversy is nothing new in the world and works of Louisa May Alcott, and her popularity continues unabated. *Little Women* has been translated into at least fifty languages. Louisa has been honored on two U.S. postage stamps—first in 1940 and again in 1994. In 1989, young readers of *Cobblestone*, a popular children's history magazine, voted Louisa May Alcott as person of the year.

New versions of *Little Women* continue to be released in forms that Louisa couldn't even have imagined when she wrote her most famous story. In 1995, a CD-ROM version of *Little Women* was released. Fans can also read Louisa's books on World Wide Web sites on the Internet. Some fans even put their own writings about Louisa and her stories on the Internet for other Louisa fans to share. In 1997, author Susan Beth Pfeffer and Delacorte Press released a new series based on the March sisters. *Portraits of Little Women* introduce readers to Meg, Jo, Beth, and Amy, each at age 10. The four hardcover books each include a craft activity and a recipe. *Little Women* has come a long way since the modest book was published 130 years ago.

Each year, about 55,000 people visit Orchard House, which has become a Concord museum. After Louisa's death, Margaret Sidney, author of the popular children's book *The Five Little Peppers and How They Grew,* purchased the house and then sold it to the Concord Women's Club in 1910. It was opened as a museum the following year, with donations sent from around the world to help restore the home and build a tribute to one of Concord's most beloved citizens. Friends and relatives shared their memories of how Orchard House looked during the time the Alcotts lived there, so that it could be restored as authentically as possible.

Visitors to Orchard House may participate in living history programs that bring Louisa's times and work to life. Costumed actors and visitors play games, sing, and have tea in the parlor. Tourists can also write a story with Louisa, take an art lesson with May, and learn how to keep a diary just as Louisa did. Each spring, Louisa's relatives take part in the annual reenactment of Anna's marriage to John Pratt.

As new generations of readers discover *Little Women* and Louisa's other works, they honor the ambitious and dedicated writer who, in her determination to serve her family, succeeded in serving millions of readers worldwide.

SOURCES

7   Madeleine Stern, *Louisa May Alcott at 150: A Writer's Progress* (Provo, Utah: Friends of the Brigham Young University Library Newsletter, 1984), 70.

9   Bronson Alcott, *The Journals of Bronson Alcott*, ed. Odell Shepard (Boston: Little, Brown, 1938), 47.

12–13   Louisa May Alcott, "Recollections of my Childhood," *The Youth's Companion*, May 24, 1888, 261.

13   Ibid.

14   Ibid.

22   Bronson Alcott, *The Journals of Bronson Alcott*, 133.

22   Louisa May Alcott, "Recollections of my Childhood," 261.

24   Madeleine B. Stern, *Louisa May Alcott* (Norman, Okla.: University of Oklahoma Press, 1950), 23.

29   Louisa May Alcott, *The Journals of Louisa May Alcott*, ed. Joel Myerson, Daniel Shealy, and Madeline B. Stern (Boston: Little, Brown, 1987), 4.

30   Bronson Alcott, *The Journals of Bronson Alcott*, 153.

32   Myerson, Shealy, and Stern, *The Journals of Louisa May Alcott*, 45.

33   Ibid.

34   Ibid.

34   Ibid.

35   Ibid., 46.

35   Ibid., 47.

35   Ibid., 45.

37–38   Ibid., 47.

39   Louisa May Alcott, "Transcendental Wild Oats," in *Bronson Alcott's Fruitlands*, ed. Clara Endicott Sears (Philadelphia: Porcupine Press, 1975), 155.

39   Louisa May Alcott, *The Journals of Louisa May Alcott*, 48.

42   Bronson Alcott, *The Journals of Bronson Alcott*, 157.

45   Louisa May Alcott, *The Journals of Louisa May Alcott*, 57.

46   Louisa May Alcott, *The Selected Letters of Louisa May Alcott*, ed. Joel Myerson, Daniel Shealy, and Madeline B. Stern (Boston: Little, Brown, 1987), 4.

46   Louisa May Alcott, *The Journals of Louisa May Alcott*, 56.

46–47   Ibid., 54–55.

47   Clara Gowing, *The Alcotts as I Knew Them* (Boston: C.M. Clark, 1909), 7.

48   Louisa May Alcott, "Recollections of my Childhood," 261.
50–51 Ibid.
51   Louisa May Alcott, *The Selected Letters of Louisa May Alcott*, 6.
51   Louisa May Alcott, *The Journals of Louisa May Alcott*, 59.
51   Ibid.
52   Madelon Bedell, *The Alcotts: Biography of a Family* (New York: Clarkson Potter, 1980), 239.
55   Louisa May Alcott, "Recollections of my Childhood," 261.
56   Louisa May Alcott, *The Journals of Louisa May Alcott*, 61.
57   Ibid.
59   Ibid., 65.
60   Ibid., 68.
60   Louisa May Alcott, *The Selected Letters of Louisa May Alcott*, 26.
60   Louisa May Alcott, *The Journals of Louisa May Alcott*, 78.
61   *Boston Evening Transcript*, December 19, 1854.
61   Louisa May Alcott, *The Journals of Louisa May Alcott*, 73.
61   Ibid., 99.
62   Louisa May Alcott, *The Journals of Louisa May Alcott*, 74.
62   Ibid., 75.
63   Ibid.
63   Ibid.
66   Ibid., 82.
66   Louisa May Alcott, *The Selected Letters of Louisa May Alcott*, 119.
67   Louisa May Alcott, *The Journals of Louisa May Alcott*, 79.
67   Louisa May Alcott, *The Selected Letters of Louisa May Alcott*, 117.
67   Louisa May Alcott, *The Journals of Louisa May Alcott*, 79.
67   Ibid.
67   Ibid.
68–69 Ibid., 80.
69   Ibid., 85.
69   Ibid., 85.
71   Ibid., 89.
71   "The Alcotts," *The Literary World*, March 17, 1888, 88.
71   "Louisa May Alcott: Her Life, Letters, and Journals," *The Athenaeum*, November 9, 1889, 632.
72   Louisa May Alcott, *The Journals of Louisa May Alcott*, 184.
74   Ibid., 105.
75   Ibid., 110.
77–78 Ibid.

78   Ibid.
78   Ibid., 113.
78–79 Ibid., 114.
80   Ibid.
81   Ibid., 114.
81   Ibid.
82   Ibid., 115.
84   Ibid., 117.
84–85 Louisa May Alcott, *Hospital Sketches* (New York: Hurst &
     Company, 1863), 30.
86   Louisa May Alcott, *The Journals of Louisa May Alcott*, 121.
87   Henry James, "Miss Alcott's Moods," *The North American
     Review,* July, 1865, 281.
89   Louisa May Alcott, *The Journals of Louisa May Alcott*, 158.
90   Ibid., 162.
90   Louisa May Alcott, *The Selected Letters of Louisa May Alcott,*
     113.
90   Louisa May Alcott, *The Journals of Louisa May Alcott*, 164.
91   Louisa May Alcott, *The Selected Letters of Louisa May Alcott,*
     113.
91   Louisa May Alcott, *The Journals of Louisa May Alcott*, 163.
92   Ibid., 165.
92   Ibid.
92   Ibid., 166.
92   Ibid., 165.
92–93 Ibid.
93   Louisa May Alcott, *Little Women: Parts I and II* (Boston:
     Little, Brown, and Co., 1920), 10.
93   Ibid., 47.
94   Alma J. Payne, *Louisa May Alcott: A Reference Guide* (Boston:
     G.K. Hall, 1980), xv.
95   Louisa May Alcott, *Little Women: Parts I and II*, 94–95.
96–97 Ibid., 45.
97–98 Ibid., 115.
98   Louisa May Alcott, *The Journals of Louisa May Alcott,* 166.
99   Ibid.
100 "The Alcotts," *The Literary World,* March 17, 1888, 88.
100 "Little Women," *Godey's Lady's Book and Magazine,* December,
     1868, 546.
101 Mather Collection, State Historical Society of Iowa, Iowa City.
101 Louisa May Alcott, *The Journals of Louisa May Alcott*, 167.
101 Ibid.
103 Ibid., 171.

103   Ibid.
103   Ibid.
104   Ibid., 183.
104   Ibid.
106   Ibid., 216.
106   Ibid., 233.
106   Ibid., 216.
106   Louisa May Alcott, *The Selected Letters of Louisa May Alcott*, 238.
107   Ibid., 252.
109   Ibid., 177.
109   Louisa May Alcott, *Work: A Story of Experience* (Boston: Roberts Brothers, 1873), 2.
109   Ibid., dedication page.
111   Ibid., 179.
111   Louisa May Alcott, *The Journals of Louisa May Alcott*, 211.
114   Ibid., 333.

BIBLIOGRAPHY

WRITINGS OF LOUISA MAY ALCOTT

Behind A Mask: The Unknown Thrillers of Louisa May Alcott. Ed. Madeleine Stern. New York: William Morrow, 1975.
Hospital Sketches. New York: Hurst & Company, 1863.
The Inheritance. New York: Dutton, 1997.
The Journals of Louisa May Alcott. Ed. Joel Myerson, Daniel Shealy, and Madeleine B. Stern. Boston: Little, Brown, 1987.
Little Women: Parts I and II. Boston: Little, Brown, 1920.
"Recollections of my Childhood." *The Youth's Companion,* May 24, 1888.
The Selected Letters of Louisa May Alcott. Ed. Joel Myerson, Daniel Shealy, and Madeleine B. Stern. Boston: Little, Brown, 1987.
"Transcendental Wild Oats." In *Bronson Alcott's Fruitlands,* ed. Clara Endicott Sears. Philadelphia: Porcupine Press, 1975.
Work: A Story of Experience. Boston: Roberts Brothers, 1873.

OTHER BOOK SOURCES

Alcott, A. Bronson. *The Journals of Bronson Alcott.* Ed. Odell Shepard. Boston: Little, Brown, 1938.
Alcott, A. Bronson. *The Letters of A. Bronson Alcott.* Ed. Richard L. Herrnstadt. Ames, Iowa: Iowa State University Press, 1969.
Bedell, Madelon. *The Alcotts: Biography of a Family.* New York: Clarkson N. Potter, 1980.
Boylan, Anne M. "Growing up Female in Young America, 1800–1860." In *American Childhood: A Research Guide and Historical Handbook.* Westport, Conn.: Greenwood Press, 1985.
Brooks, Paul. *The People of Concord: One Year in the Flowering of New England.* Chester, Conn.: Globe Pequot Press, 1990.
Butts, Freeman R. *Public Education in the United States: From Revolution to Reform.* New York: Holt, Rinehart & Wilson, 1978.
Clement, Richard W. *The Book in America.* Golden, Colo.: Fulcrum, 1996.
Dahlstrand, Frederick C. *Amos Bronson Alcott: An Intellectual Biography.* London: Fairleigh Dickinson University Press, 1982.
Finklestein, Barbara. "The Reconstruction of Childhood in the United States," in *American Childhood: A Research Guide and Historical Handbook.* Westport, Conn.: Greenwood Press, 1985.
Gowing, Clara. *The Alcotts as I Knew Them.* Boston: C.M. Clark, 1909.
Hoy, Suellen. *Chasing Dirt: The American Pursuit of Cleanliness.* New York: Oxford University Press, 1995.
Johnston, Norma. *Louisa May: The World and Works of Louisa May Alcott.* New York: Four Winds Press, 1991.
Meigs, Cornelia. *Invincible Louisa: The Story of the Author of Little Women.* Boston: Little, Brown, 1933.
Payne, Alma J. *Louisa May Alcott: A Reference Guide.* Boston: G.K., 1980.

Rusk, Ralph L. *The Life of Ralph Waldo Emerson*. New York: College University Press, 1949.
Saxton, Martha. *Louisa May: A Modern Biography of Louisa May Alcott*. Boston: Houghton Mifflin, 1977.
Scott Publishing Company. *1998 Standard Postage Stamp Catalogue*, Volume 1. Sidney, Ohio: Scott, 1997.
Solton, Lee, and Edward Stevens. *The Rise of Literacy and the Common School in the United States: A Socioeconomic Analysis to 1870*. Chicago: University of Chicago Press, 1981.
Stern, Madeleine. *Louisa May Alcott at 150: A Writer's Progress*. Provo, Utah: Friends of the Brigham Young University Library Newsletter, 1984.
Street, Douglas, ed. *Children's Novels and the Movies*. New York: Frederick Ungar, 1983.
Strickland, Charles. *Victorian Domesticity: Families in the Life and Art of Louisa May Alcott*. University, Alab.: University of Alabama Press, 1985.

MAGAZINE AND NEWSPAPER ARTICLES (NO AUTHORS LISTED)

"The Alcotts." *The Literary World*, March 17, 1888.
"The Alcotts." *The Athenaeum*, March 24, 1888, 372-373.
"Little Women." *Godey's Lady's Book and Magazine*. December, 1868.
"Little Women." *School Library Journal*. July, 1995, vol. 41, no. 7, 34.
"Louisa M. Alcott." *Blackwoods*, 870-871.
"Louisa May Alcott: Her Life, Letters, and Journals." *The Athenaeum*, November 9, 1889.
"Person of the Year Award." *Cobblestone*, June, 1989, 43.
"Two New England Women." *Atlantic Monthly*, March, 1890, 420-421.
"A Yankee Pythagoras." *The North American Review*, July, 1888, 345-346.

MAGAZINE AND NEWSPAPER ARTICLES (AUTHORS LISTED)

Anderson, William T. "Louisa May Alcott." *American History Illustrated*, March, 1988, 24-37, 48.
Hawthorne, Julian. "The Woman Who Wrote Little Women." *The Ladies' Home Journal*, October, 1922, 25+.
James, Henry. "Miss Alcott's Moods." *The North American Review*, July, 1865, 276-281.
Lurie, Alison. "She Had it All." *The New York Review of Books*, March 2, 1995, 5.
Porter, Maria S. "Recollections of Louisa May Alcott." *The New England Magazine*, March, 1892, 3-19.
Schickel, Richard. "Cinema: Transcendental Meditation." *Time*, December 19, 1994, 74.
Stern, Madeleine B. "Louisa May Alcott: Civil War Nurse." *Americana*, April, 1943, 296-322.
Streff, Sally. "Littler Literature." *Miami Herald*, February 20, 1995, 1A+.

UNPUBLISHED MANUSCRIPTS

Mather Collection, State Historical Society of Iowa, Iowa City.

INDEX

ABOUT THE AUTHOR

Amy Ruth is a regular contribu-
tor to newspapers and magazines
nationwide. In 1997, she completed
a picture book about President
Herbert Hoover, commissioned by
the Herbert Hoover Presidential
Library and Museum in West
Branch, Iowa. She has a bache-
lor's degree in English from Virginia Commonwealth University in Richmond,
Virginia, and a master's degree in journalism from the
University of Iowa, Iowa City. She and her husband,
writer/photographer Jim Meisner, live in Richmond,
Virginia, and often collaborate on projects.

PHOTO ACKNOWLEDGMENTS

The photographs and illustrations are reproduced with the permission of Houghton Library, Harvard University, p. 9; Concord
Free Public Library, pp. 13, 19, 44, 49, 50, 91, 102, 113; Corbis,
pp. 14, 64, 70, 74, 80; Corbis-Bettmann, pp. 40, 63, 88, 94, 96;
Louisa May Alcott Memorial Association, pp. 2, 16, 20, 23, 54, 59,
62, 76, 99, 105, 110; National Archives, p. 79; Library of Congress,
p. 43; The Norman Rockwell Museum at Stockbridge, pp. 6, 68;
Archive Photos, p. 37; © David Wade, pp. 26, 70, 83, 114; Independent Picture Service, p. 31; Jim Meisner, p. 128. Front cover
photograph: Louisa May Alcott Memorial Association. Back cover
photograph: Corbis.